D1460086

AIR WAR FLANDERS-1918

AIR WAR FLANDERS-1918

Airlife

First published in the UK in 1998
by Airlife Publishing Ltd

British Library Cataloguing-in-Publication Data
A catalogue record for this book
is available from the British Library

ISBN 1 84037 004 1

Typeset by Servis Filmsetting Ltd, Manchester, England
Printed in England by Butler & Tanner Ltd, Frome and London

Airlife Publishing Ltd
101 Longden Road, Shrewsbury, SY3 9EB, England

Contents

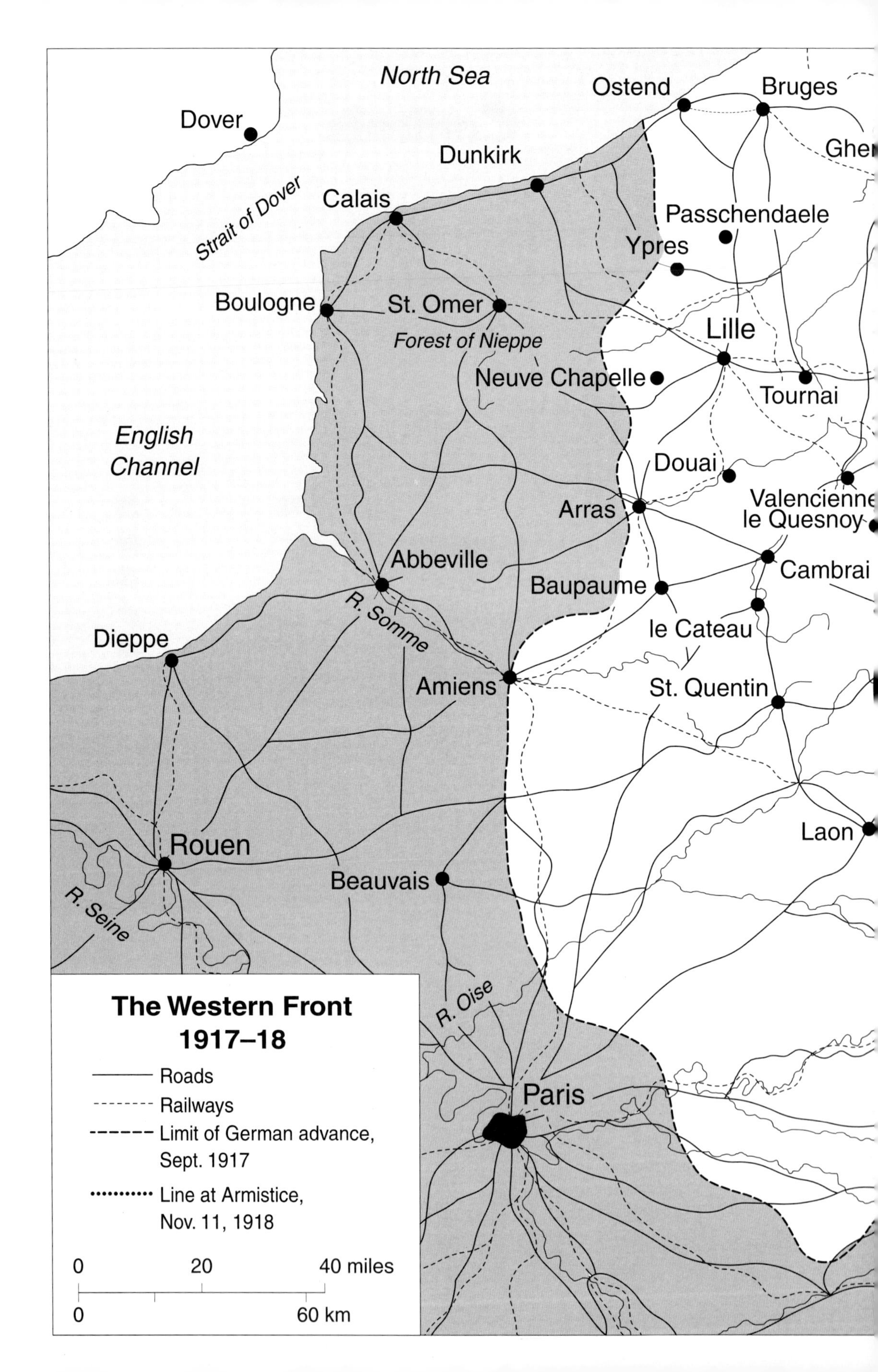
North Sea
Dover
Strait of Dover
Ostend
Bruges
Dunkirk
Calais
Passchendaele
Ypres
Boulogne
St. Omer
Forest of Nieppe
Lille
Neuve Chapelle
Tournai
English Channel
Douai
Arras
Valencienne
le Quesnoy
Abbeville
Cambrai
Baupaume
R. Somme
le Cateau
Dieppe
Amiens
St. Quentin
Laon
Rouen
Beauvais
R. Seine
R. Oise
Paris
The Western Front 1917–18
Roads
Railways
Limit of German advance, Sept. 1917
Line at Armistice, Nov. 11, 1918
0
20
40 miles
0
60 km

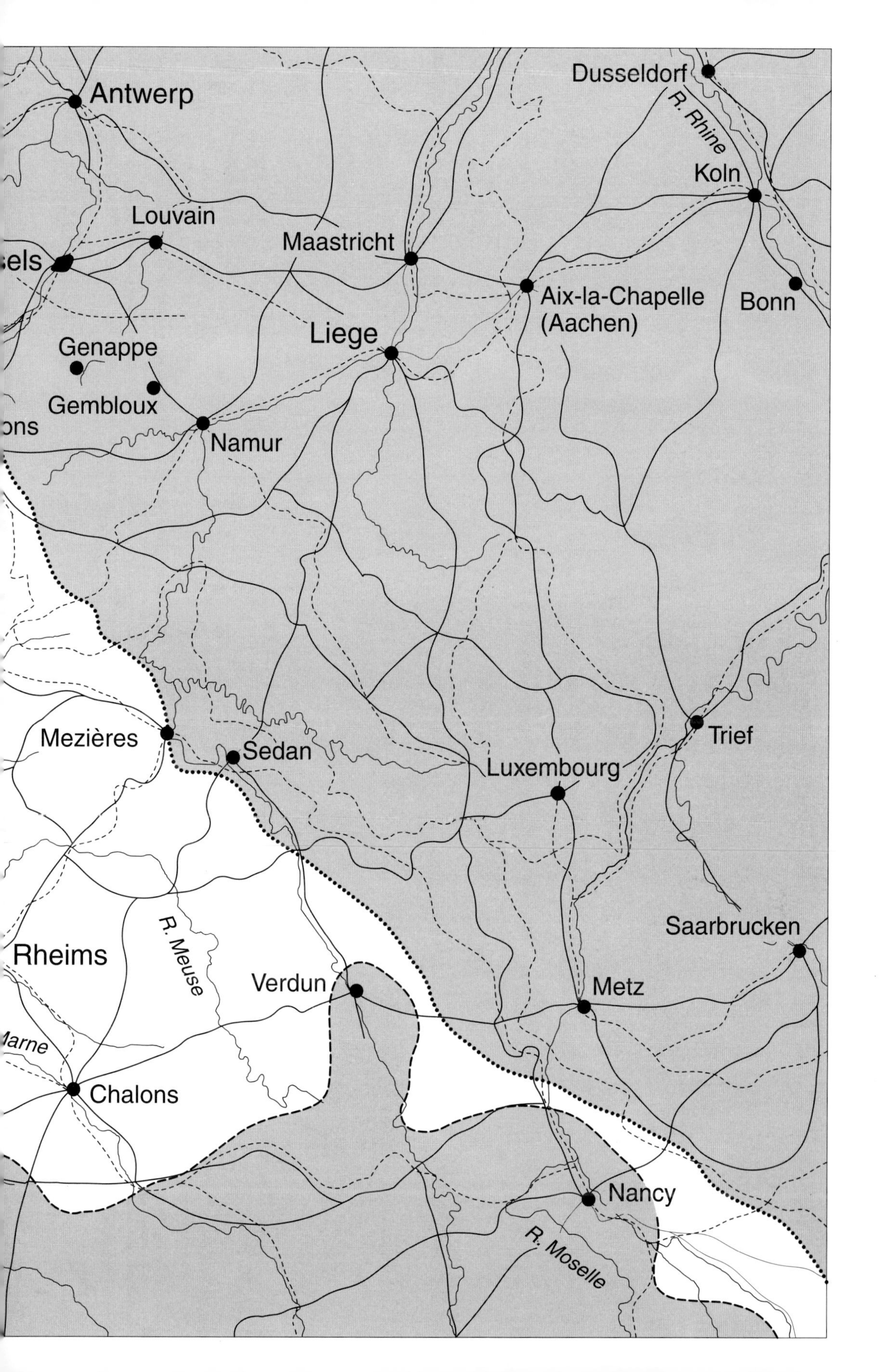

Antwerp
Dusseldorf
R. Rhine
Koln
Louvain
Maastricht
sels
Aix-la-Chapelle
(Aachen)
Bonn
Liege
Genappe
Gembloux
ons
Namur
Mezières
Sedan
Trief
Luxembourg
Saarbrucken
R. Meuse
Rheims
Verdun
Metz
Marne
Chalons
Nancy
R. Moselle

Chapter One
Flanders, 1917: a fall of aces

Above: SE 5as of No 40 Squadron.

'The May evening is heavy with threatening masses of cumulus cloud, majestic skyscapes, solid-looking as snow mountains, fraught with caves and valleys, rifts and ravines . . . Steadily the body of scouts rises higher and higher, threading its way between the cloud precipices. Sometimes, below, the streets of a village, the corner of a wood, a few dark figures moving, glides into view like a slide into a lantern and is then hidden again . . .

'A red light curls up from the leader's cockpit and falls away. Action! He alters direction slightly, and the patrol, shifting throttle and rudder, keep close like a pack of hounds on the scent. He has seen, and they see soon, six scouts three thousand feet below. Black crosses! It seems interminable till the eleven come within diving distance. The pilots nurse their engines, hard-minded and set, test their guns and watch their indicators. At last the leader sways sideways, as a signal that each should take his man, and suddenly drops . . .'

That was how RFC pilot Cecil Lewis, in his book *Sagittarius Rising*, described the start of the battle that was to cost the life of Britain's ace of aces, Captain Albert Ball, on that evening of 7 May, 1917. Ball, a flight commander with No 56 Squadron, the holder of the DSO and two Bars, plus the MC, had taken off a while earlier from Vert Galand to carry out an offensive patrol in the direction of Douai aerodrome, the base of *Jagdstaffel* 11, which was commanded by a German officer who was already legendary: Manfred von Richthofen.

As the fight was joined it began to rain, cutting down the visibility. The section leaders of No 56 Squadron, which had only arrived in France with its SE 5 scouts a month earlier, tried hard to hold their men together, but in the confusion of the dogfight the squadron became split up. Some of the pilots broke away and made for home; others, including Ball, headed for a prearranged rendezvous over Arras. There, Ball joined up with another flight commander named Crowe and the two continued their patrol, joined by a lone SPAD.

Near Loos, Ball suddenly fired off a couple of signal flares and dived on a red-and-yellow Fokker Triplane, following it into a cloud. It was the last time that he was seen alive. Of the eleven SE 5s that had set out, only five returned to base.

The credit for Albert Ball's death was claimed by Lothar von Richthofen, Manfred's brother. The claim was false, and to this day mystery surrounds the RFC pilot's demise. He was either shot down by a machine-gun mounted on a church steeple, or became disorientated in low cloud and went out of control. The Germans buried him near Lille, and dropped a message to that effect over No 56 Squadron's aerodrome. A month later, it was announced that Ball had been posthumously awarded the Victoria Cross. His score of enemy aircraft destroyed at the time of death was forty-seven; he was twenty-two years old.

Albert Ball was survived for a few more months by his closest Allied rival, Lt Georges Guynemer of *Escadrille* SPA.3. The unit was known as *L'Escadrille des Cigognes* – the Stork Squadron – and its SPAD S VII scouts carried a white marabou insignia on their fuselage sides. For a while Ball and Guynemer were running neck-and-neck; in fact, at the beginning of May 1917 Ball had surpassed the French pilot's total, and there was much speculation about whether he would catch up with Manfred von Richthofen, who then had fifty-two victories.

On 6 September 1917 Guynemer, now a captain, shot down his fifty-fourth victim. Five days later, accompanied by Lt Bozon-Verduraz, he took off on his last patrol. Bozon-Verduraz' combat report tells the terse story:

> 'At 09.25, together with *Capitaine* Guynemer, attacked an enemy two-seater over the lines at Poelcapelle. Made one pass and fired thirty rounds. *Capitaine* Guynemer continued to pursue the enemy as I was obliged to break off to avoid eight single-seaters, which were preparing to attack me. I did not see *Capitaine* Guynemer again. At 10.20, attacked a two-seater at 5,900 metres over Poperinghe. Fired ten rounds at point-blank range, then gun jammed. Pursued the enemy, but was unable to clear the stoppage and returned to base.'

Below: SPAD flown by Georges Guynemer.

It was three days before the French authorities had an inkling of what had happened to Guynemer; a German newspaper carried a report stating that the French ace had been shot down by a *Hauptmann* Wissemann, but it was to be another month before the news was officially confirmed. In response to a note sent via the Spanish Embassy, the Department of Foreign Affairs in Berlin issued the following statement:

> 'Captain Guynemer fell in the course of an air fight at 10.00 am on 11 September last, close to Cemetery of Honour No 11 to the south of Poelcapelle. A medical examination revealed that the index finger of the left hand had been shot away, and that the cause of death was a bullet in the head.'

After a brief examination by a German patrol, Guynemer's body was left in the wreckage until it could be recovered safely. Before this could be done, however, the British artillery laid down a heavy barrage on the area where Guynemer's aircraft had come down, completely obliterating all trace of the machine and its pilot.

About a week after Guynemer's death, the man who claimed to have shot him down wrote home to his family, telling them not to worry about him, and that never again was he likely to meet an adversary who was half as dangerous as Guynemer. Only nineteen days later, Wissemann was himself shot down and killed by a man who was destined to emerge from the holocaust of the 1914–18 War as the top-scoring Allied fighter pilot. His name was René Fonck.

Fonck, who had scored his first victories over the Somme battleground in 1916, and who had joined the *Cigognes* in April of the following year, soon began to consolidate his position as one of Frances best fighter pilots. In October 1917, in the course of a total sortie time of thirteen and a half hours, he destroyed ten enemy aircraft. His tactics were simple. He would cruise at high altitude, so that he was almost always above his opponents; then, choosing his moment carefully, he would use his height and speed advantage to gain surprise. His aim was excellent, and a single firing pass on the dive was usually

Below: Werner Voss, the 'Hussar of Krefeld', beside his Fokker Triplane.

enough to send down his enemy. By the end of 1917 Fonck's score stood at nineteen enemy aircraft destroyed, placing him equal third with two other talented pilots, *Capitaines* Albert Deullin and Georges Madon. In second place was *Capitaine* Alfred Heurtaux, with twenty-one, and leading the field was Lt Charles Nungesser, the senior surviving French pilot, with thirty victories.

On the German side, the second top-scoring ace after Manfred von Richthofen was *Leutnant* Werner Voss of *Jagdstaffel* 10, who had destroyed forty-seven Allied aircraft by the beginning of September 1917. Voss was due to go on leave with his two brothers, and on 23 September they arrived at his aerodrome, intending to travel back to Germany together. Before departing, Voss decided to go out on an offensive patrol, flying a Fokker Triplane. This type had first made its appearance on the Western Front early in September and, in the hands of an experienced pilot, was a formidable fighting machine. But even experienced pilots were not invincible; *Leutnant* Kurt Wolff, the commander of *Jagdstaffel* 11 and an ace with thirty-three victories, had been shot down and killed in a Triplane on 5 September by Flight Sub-Lt N. MacGregor of No 10 (Naval) Squadron, flying a Sopwith Camel.

Soon after starting his patrol, Werner Voss shot down an Airco DH 4, heading back towards the front line after a sortie, but then he developed engine trouble and returned to base, exchanging his Triplane for another. At 6.00 pm, in poor visibility, he took off again accompanied by two Albatros Scouts, which still formed the main equipment of *Jasta* 11. Approaching the front line, they saw an air battle in progress between a variety of British and German aircraft, including the SE 5s of No 60 Squadron. Voss immediately manoeuvred into position to attack one of these, which was flown by Lt H.A. Hamersley and which had become separated from the rest.

Twenty minutes earlier, six SE 5s of 'B' Flight, No 56 Squadron, had taken off from their airfield at Estrée Blanche. The flight was led by Captain James B. McCudden, who was accompanied by Lts Gerald Bowman, Arthur Rhys-Davids, Keith Muspratt, Richard Maybery and R.T.C. Hoidge. The flight attacked an enemy two-seater, which was shot down by McCudden, and then reformed and climbed to attack a formation of six Albatros Scouts, flying just below the cloud base. At that moment, McCudden spotted Hamersley's lone SE 5, pursued by Voss, somewhat lower down. Abandoning the Albatros formation, he went after the Triplane in a diving turn, followed by Arthur Rhys-Davids.

The pair closed in rapidly on the German, one on either side, taking it in turns to fire in short bursts. Voss, with four more SE 5s coming down hard and already effectively boxed in, took the only course of action open to him. Using the Fokker's remarkable manoeuvrability to the fullest advantage, he decided to fight his attackers by turning to face them, doubtless hoping that he could hold them at bay until reinforcements arrived.

The manoeuvre took McCudden completely by surprise, as he wrote later.

> 'To my amazement he kicked on full rudder without bank, pulled his nose up slightly, gave me a burst while he was skidding sideways, and then kicked on opposite rudder before the results of this amazing stunt appeared to have any effect on the controllability of his machine.'

With a burst of gunfire through his wing, the startled McCudden broke away sharply. At that moment, a red-nosed Albatros D V joined the battle. Its pilot, almost as skilful as Voss himself, took on the task of protecting Voss's tail, and with his assistance the German ace abandoned his purely defensive tactics and got in some damaging shots at the SEs that were trying to out-turn him. The battle went on for a full ten minutes, but the help the German pilots were

Above: Arthur Rhys-Davids, the RFC pilot who shot down Voss.

counting on never arrived, and the outcome was inevitable. The combat report of Lt Rhys-Davids describes the last frantic minutes of the fight:

'The red-nosed Albatros and the triplane fought magificently. I got in several bursts at the triplane without apparent effect, and twice placed a new drum on my Lewis gun. Eventually I got east of and slightly above the triplane and made for it, getting in a whole Lewis drum and a corresponding number of rounds from my Vickers. He made an attempt to turn in and we were so close that I was certain that we would collide. He passed my starboard wing by inches and went down. I zoomed, and saw him next with his engine apparently out, gliding east. I dived again and got one shot out of my Vickers. I reloaded, keeping in the dive, and got in another good burst, the triplane effecting a slight starboard turn, still going down. I had now overshot him, but never saw him again.'

McCudden, who had temporarily broken off the fight to change an ammunition drum, witnessed the Triplane's last moments. He noted that it seemed to stagger and then fly erratically for a short time before going into a steep dive, streaming smoke, and exploding on impact with the ground. A few moments later the red-nosed Albatros also went down in flames.

Later, James McCudden wrote of Voss: 'His flying was wonderful, his courage magnificent, and in my opinion he was the bravest German airman whom it has been my privilege to see fight.' But perhaps the feelings of the British pilots were best summed up by young Rhys-Davids himself, the man who had ended the career of the 'Hussar of Krefeld', as Voss was nicknamed. As his colleagues gathered around to congratulate him, he shook his head and murmured, as he set his glass aside: 'Oh, if only I could have brought him down alive!'

* * *

Such were the young men who, in 1917, brought new skills and tactics to the science of air warfare, building on earlier lessons bought at terrible cost by their predecessors of 1915–16. The losses sustained by the RFC by the end of 1916 were, in fact, so severe that they brought about a manpower crisis, so that early in 1917 the War Office found it necessary to order regimental commanders to appeal for volunteers for transfer to the flying service to train as pilots and observers. Hundreds came forward, many for no reason other than that they preferred to face death in the air rather than in the mud and slime of the trenches, and at the same time the first Commonwealth and Dominion volunteers also began to arrive. They were led by the Canadians, who, by special arrangement with the United States, had done most of their flying training in Texas and, unlike many of their British contemporaries, already possessed a considerable degree of skill.

The flow of fresh personnel into the RFC during the early months of 1917 did much to raise morale as the Corps prepared to support the planned spring offensives. The primary tasks of the RFC were, as always, reconnaissance and artillery observation, but the observation aircraft had to be protected from the attentions of enemy scouts, and this requirement had in turn given rise to the rapid development of fighter tactics that were designed to secure air superiority over an area of considerable depth behind the enemy lines while the observation machines went about their business.

The first Allied offensive of 1917 involved a major French attack on the Aisne while the British pinned down a large part of the enemy forces in the north, the main objective in their sector being the capture of Vimy Ridge. The offensive began on 17 March and ended on 4 April. The First and Third British Armies were supported by twenty-five RFC squadrons, about half of them equipped with single-seat fighters. It was during this battle that a new British combat aircraft, the Bristol F.2A Fighter, made its operational debut. Fifty F.2As were built; powered by a 190 hp Rolls-Royce Falcon engine giving it a top speed of around 115 mph and armed with a centrally-mounted forward-firing Vickers gun and a single Lewis mounted in the rear cockpit, the first examples arriving in France with No 48 Squadron towards the end of March.

The squadron had only six Bristols in operation at the time of its arrival at its new base, Bellevue, and they were rushed into action before their pilots had time to get used to them or to develop proper tactics with them. At first they were flown like earlier two-seaters, orientated around the observer's gun as the primary weapon, and losses were heavy. During their first patrol on 5 April 1917, six Bristols led by No 48 Squadron's CO, Major W. Leefe

Below: Bristol F.2B Fighter. At first thought easy prey by the Germans, it soon proved its worth.

Above: Bristol Fighters in flight.

Robinson VC (who had earlier distinguished himself by shooting down the German Schütte-Lanz airship SL11 at Cuffley on 2 September 1916) encountered five Albatros D IIs led by Manfred von Richthofen. The British pilots adopted the standard two-seater tactic of turning their backs on the enemy to allow their observers to bring their guns to bear. It was a serious mistake, and four of the six – including Leefe Robinson, who spent the rest of the war in a prison camp – were shot down.

Later, in an interview with a Berlin newspaper, Richthofen was openly contemptuous of the British machine, with the result that many German pilots came to regard the Bristol Fighter as easy game – with fatal consequences to themselves. When flown offensively, in the same way as a single-seat fighter, it proved to be a superb weapon and went on to log a formidable record of success in action. Several hundred Bristol Fighters were ordered in 1917, these being the F.2B version with a 220 hp Falcon II or 275 hp Falcon III engine, wide-span tailplane, modified lower wing centre section and an improved view from the front cockpit. The F.2B eventually served with six RFC squadrons – Nos 11, 20, 22, 48, 62 and 88 – on the Western Front, as well as with No 67 (Australian) Squadron in Palestine, No 139 Squadron in Italy, and with Nos 33, 36, 76 and 141 on home defence duties in the United Kingdom. The pilot who perhaps did most to vindicate the Bristol Fighter was a Canadian, Lt Andrew McKeever, who destroyed thirty enemy aircraft while flying F.2Bs, his various observers shooting down eleven more.

Another new type to enter RFC service in the spring of 1917 was the SE 5 single-seat scout, which was delivered to No 56 Squadron in March. Powered by a 150 hp Hispano-Suiza engine, the aircraft had a maximum speed of 120 mph. Armament comprised a synchronised Vickers gun firing through the propeller and a drum-fed Lewis mounted over the wing centre section. Although less manoeuvrable than either the French-built Nieuports and SPADs, the SE 5 was faster and had an excellent rate of climb, enabling it to hold its own in combat with the latest German fighter types. The SE 5s of No 56 Squadron flew their first operational patrol on 22 April 1917.

The original SE 5 was followed into service, in June 1917, by the SE 5a, with a 200 hp Hispano-Suiza engine. The type was first issued to Nos 56, 40 and 60 Squadrons, in that order, and by the end of the year had been delivered to Nos 24, 41, 68 and 84. Deliveries were slowed by an acute shortage of engines, but the pilots of the units that did receive the SE 5a were full of praise for the aircraft's fine flying qualities, physical strength and performance. It is probably no exaggeration to say that, in most respects, the SE 5a was the Spitfire of the First World War.

It certainly had none of the vicious tendencies of the Sopwith Camel – although in fairness, once the Camel had been thoroughly mastered it was a superb fighting machine, and in fact it was to be credited with the destruction of more enemy aircraft than any other Allied type before the conflict ended. Early production Camels were powered either by the 130 hp Clerget 9B or the 150 hp Bentley BR 1 rotary engine, but subsequent aircraft were fitted with either the Clerget or the 110 hp Le Rhône 9J. Armament comprised twin Vickers guns mounted in front of the cockpit, and four 20 lb Cooper bombs could be carried under the fuselage for ground attack. The first unit to receive Camels was No 4 Squadron Royal Naval Air Service, followed by No 70 Squadron RFC, both in July 1917.

Delivery of the SE 5 and the Camel came too late to prevent heavy RFC losses, which continued to mount steadily during the spring of 1917. There were three main reasons for the growing casualty rate. First, the RFC was still critically deficient in adequate combat aircraft; secondly, the prevailing westerly wind – which tended to carry the mêlée of air combat deep into enemy territory – was in the Germans' favour; and thirdly, the RFC's insistence on maintaining an offensive policy throughout, no matter what the cost, in the face of superior enemy aircraft. By April 1917 new pilots were being sent to the front with as little as seventeen

Below: SE 5a of No 40 Squadron. The pilot is Captain G.H. Lewis.

Above: Sopwith Camel B5198 of No 43 Squadron.

and a half hours' flying experience, which precipitated a vicious circle; the more inexperienced the British pilots, the higher the success rate of the German fighter squadrons. By the middle of 'Bloody April' 1917 the average life expectancy of an RFC pilot in France had dropped to two months.

During the first week of April 1917 the RFC lost seventy-five aircraft in action, mostly victims of an emerging band of tough, resolute air fighters nurtured in the traditions of Germany's first air aces and fighter tacticians, Oswald Boelcke and Max Immelmann. At their head was *Rittmeister Freiherr* Manfred von Richthofen, and other German pilots were potentially just as dangerous to the Allies: men like Bruno Lörzer, the leader of *Jagdstaffel* 26, who destroyed ten British aircraft during the Battle of Arras and who was to survive the war with forty-five victories. More than two decades later, the highly experienced Lörzer would command *Fliegerkorps* II during the Battle of Britain. Then there was Werner Voss, whose fate we have already seen; Erich Löwenhardt, who had forty victories in the spring of 1917 and who later went on to score sixteen more; Karl Allmenröder and Karl Schäfer, with thirty victories each; Kurt Wolff, with twenty-seven at the time of the Battle of Arras; Otto Bernert with twenty-six; and many others who were to be numbered among the German Flying Corps' fifty top-scorers before the end of the war.

In accordance with the German policy of concentrating their best pilots into single crack units, most of the above-named men served with Richthofen's *Jagdstaffel* 11. A *Jagdstaffel*, abbreviated to *Jasta*, usually consisted of twelve or fourteen aircraft, although later this was increased to twenty-one. In June 1917 *Jasta*s 4, 6, 10 and 11 were merged into a single *Jagdgeschwader* (Fighter Wing) under

Richthofen's command. Although patrols were still flown at *Jasta* strength, Richthofen could, in response to an increase in Allied air activity, concentrate a large number of fighter aircraft in any particular sector of the front. Moreover, the *Jagdgeschwader* was highly mobile and could be switched quickly from one part of the front to another in support of ground operations.

The principal German fighter aircraft in the spring of 1917 was the Albatros D III, which had first been issued to *Jasta* 11 in January that year. Powered by a Mercedes D III engine, it had a maximum speed of 108 mph and carried an armament of twin synchronized 7.92 mm Spandau machine-guns. By April 1917 all thirty-seven *Jasta*s at the front were equipped with either the D III or the earlier Albatros D II. However, the most widely used of all the Albatros fighters was the D V, which made its appearance in mid-1917. It was not a great improvement over the excellent D III, but it was produced in large numbers, over 1,500 serving with the *Jasta*s on the Western Front alone.

Later in the year, starting in August, some *Jasta*s also began to receive the Pfalz D III, which like the Albatros was powered by a Mercedes

Above: The Albatros D II helped to establish German air superiority in the air battles of early 1917.

Above: Albatros D IIs of *Jasta* 5.

Above: A captured Albatros D II brought down in the Allied lines.

Above: The Albatros D III, the first of the Albatros 'V-strutters,' was the best and most effective Albatros fighter produced in WWI.

Above: Albatros D V. Although the flying qualities of the D V and D Va were good, they were no great improvement over the D III.

Above: Albatros D V with a Gotha G V bomber in the background.

Below: Albatros D Va.

Below: A *Jagdstaffel* of Albatros Scouts on an airfield in Belgium.

engine and featured twin Spandau machine-guns. However, even at its peak the Pfalz fully equipped only half a dozen units, and for some reason German pilots seem to have been prejudiced against it; this attitude is hard to understand, because the Pfalz was a sturdy machine, capable of absorbing a great deal of battle damage, and it could be dived harder and faster than the Albatros.

The other new German fighter type introduced in 1917 was the Fokker Dr I Triplane. Its design was inspired by the Sopwith Triplane, an excellent and highly manoeuvrable fighter which served with Nos 1, 8, 9, 10, 11 and 12 Squadrons of the Royal Naval Air Service on the Western Front during most of 1917. The Fokker Triplane was never used in very large numbers, but it registered astonishing successes in the hands of leading German aces such as von Richthofen and Voss.

To counter the threat posed by the *Jagdgeschwader* in the summer of 1917, the RFC was forced to adopt a similar policy of concentrating its best fighter pilots and squadrons in opposition to von Richthofen wherever his squadrons appeared. These élite RFC units were the cradle of the leading British fighter aces. No 56 Squadron, for example, in addition to Albert Ball, numbered among its ranks such famous fighter pilots as Captain James McCudden, Lt Rhys-Davids, Capt Brunwin-Hales with twenty-seven victories and Capt Henry Burden with twenty-two; then there was Capt W.A. (Billy) Bishop of No 60 Squadron (and later of No 85), a Canadian who was to survive the war as the second-ranking RFC/RAF fighter ace with seventy-two victories, being narrowly beaten to the top by Major Mick Mannock, who had a score of at least seventy-four. Mannock flew with No 40 Squadron, as did two other leading fighter aces: Captain G.E.H. McElroy, a Canadian with a score of forty-six, and Major Roderic Dallas, a New Zealander, with thirty-nine.

In fact, the formation of large, concentrated fighter groups had been pioneered by the French during the Battle of the Somme in the summer of 1916, when the Cachy Group (so-called after its operational base near Amiens) came into existence under *Capitaine* Brocard of N.3 *Cigognes*. (To avoid confusion, it should be pointed out that the French squadrons bore the initial letter of the aircraft type they were flying; the *Cigognes* were using Nieuports at the time, and later, when they converted to SPADs, their designation was changed to SPA.3.) The Cachy Group comprised N.3, with Georges Guynemer as its leading pilot, and *Capitaine* Féquant's N.65, which included Charles Nungesser.

At the end of 1916 the French *Aéronautique Militaire* possessed three *Groupes de Combat*: GC 11 under *Commandant* Le Révérend, GC 12 under *Commandant* Brocard, and GC 13 under *Commandant* Féquant. Eleven more would be formed before the end of hostilities. Each *Groupe*

Above: Captain G.E.H. McElroy, the Canadian ace with 46 victories.

Above: A Pfalz D III Scout. Unlike the Albatros, the Pfalz was not prone to structural failure.

comprised four *Escadrilles*, each with fifteen aircraft and fifteen pilots. The *Groupes de Combat* came under the orders of the French army commanders and, like their Royal Flying Corps counterparts, had the task of establishing air superiority and protecting observation aircraft. In 1917, mixed units of fighters and bombers were employed in carrying out offensive operations.

The aircraft on which most of the French aces cut their teeth was the Nieuport 11C-1 Bébé, which entered service in the summer of 1915 and which was also used in some numbers by the RFC and RNAS. It was this little aircraft which helped to redress the balance of power following the appearance over the Western Front of the Fokker E III Monoplane, with its synchronized machine-gun firing through the propeller. The Bébé was followed into service, in May 1916, by the Nieuport 17C-1, which equipped *Escadrilles* N.3, N.38, N.55, N.57, N.65 and N.103. It also served with eight RNAS and five RFC squadrons.

In the autumn of 1916 many *Escadrilles* began to equip with a new fighter type, the SPAD (*Société Pour Aviation et ses Dérivées*) VII. Although less manoeuvrable than the Nieuport types, the SPAD VII was a strong, stable gun platform with a top speed of 119 mph and an excellent rate of climb. The SPAD VII was also used by the RFC and RNAS, and filled a crucial gap at a time when many units were still equipped with ageing and vulnerable aircraft.

In May 1917, however, the French *Escadrilles de Chasse* began to standardize on a new type, the SPAD XIII. Like its predecessor, it was an excellent gun platform and was extremely strong, although it was tricky to fly at low speeds. Powered by a Hispano-Suiza 8Ba engine and armed with two forward-firing Vickers guns, it had a maximum speed of nearly 140 mph – quite exceptional for that time – and could climb to 22,000 feet. The SPAD XIII subsequently equipped more than eighty *Escadrilles*.

Such, in broad outline, was the state of air power on both sides of the front – discounting bomber and observation types for the moment – when the British opened a new offensive in Flanders in June 1917, the main effort taking place in the Messines sector. The attack was supported by eighteen RFC squadrons with a total of 300 aircraft, about one-third of them single-seat fighters. On the first day of the offensive, 7 June, Captain W.A. Bishop of No 60 Squadron was awarded the Victoria Cross for destroying four out of seven enemy aircraft in a daring single-handed attack on an airfield near Cambrai. He was flying a Nieuport 17.

By the end of the month the RFC's reserves were sadly depleted. The situation was further aggravated by the withdrawal on 21 June of two of its best fighter squadrons, Nos 56 and 66, for home defence. This also helped to delay the re-equipment of the RFC units in France with new aircraft, notably the Sopwith Camel.

For the RFC crews, stretched to their utmost during July, it was some consolation to know that von Richthofen was out of action for a time. On 6 July, forty fighters of the Richthofen *Geschwader* had attacked six FE 2ds of No 20 Squadron, escorted by four Sopwith Triplanes of No 10 Squadron RNAS; two FEs were shot down, but an observer in another – 2nd Lt E.A. Woodbridge – got in a good burst at Richthofen's red Albatros and sent it down to make a forced landing. Richthofen was wounded in the head.

The days before the third battle of Ypres,

Below: The Nieuport 11C-1 was the aircraft on which many French aces scored their early victories.

Below: The SPAD VII was a strong, stable gun platform with an excellent rate of climb.

Above: Nieuport 24 flown by Charles Nungesser (standing with his back to the camera).

which opened on 31 July, were marked by intense air activity on both sides. At this time the combined strength of the RFC, RNAS, *Aéronautique Militaire* and the small Belgian Air Corps on the Western Front was 852 aircraft, of which 360 were fighters; the German strength was 600 machines, of which 200 were fighters.

To bolster the Allied fighter strength in Flanders, two French *Escadrilles* – including the *Cigognes* – were sent to Dunkirk from the Lorraine sector. Charles Nungesser, having experienced engine trouble, was flying alone a few hours behind the rest when he was suddenly attacked by a British aircraft near Arras and took fifteen bullets through his Nieuport. Convinced that the attacking aircraft was a captured one, flown by a German pilot, he engaged it and shot it down, landing nearby to inspect the wreck. The pilot was dead, and Nungesser, finding some identity documents on the body, discovered to his dismay that the man who had tried to kill him was in fact an RFC pilot – a very inexperienced one, as a subsequent enquiry established.

The air offensive that preceded the battle opened on 11 July, and on that first day fourteen German aircraft were destroyed for the loss of nine British. A few days later von Richthofen was back in action, his head still in bandages, and a series of massive dog fights took place between his *Jagdgeschwader* and Allied fighter formations. On the twenty-sixth, no fewer than ninety-four single-seat fighters fought one another at altitudes varying between 5,000 and 7,000 feet over Polygon Wood, and the following evening thirty Albatros fighters attacked eight FE 2ds over the same area. It was a trap; no sooner had the German fighters come down to intercept than they were attacked by fifty-nine SE 5s and Sopwith Triplanes. Nine enemy aircraft were destroyed for the loss of one SE 5.

The *Cigognes* had seldom encountered pilots of the calibre of those who made up the Richthofen *Jagdgeschwader* in the skies of Lorraine, where they had helped to defend the embattled fortress of Verdun, and they found Flanders a tough battleground. Georges Madon had an incredible escape when, flying a new SPAD XIII with which the *Escadrille* was equipping, he collided with an enemy two-seater. With his upper wing completely torn away, he spun out of control through a terrifying 10,000 feet. Literally at the last moment his aircraft miraculously righted itself before crash-landing in the Allied lines. His only injury was a broken finger.

Another ace, Lt Albert Deullin, was not so lucky. During a fight with an enemy monoplane, he took two bullets in the region of his kidneys and crash-landed, gravely wounded. He survived to fly and fight again in 1918. Alfred Heurtaux, attacking a two seater near Ypres, was hit in the thigh. Fainting through loss of blood, he went into a spin and recovered consciousness just in time to right his aircraft. He spotted a field dead ahead and went down to land on it; it turned out to be an RFC aerodrome, and the British whisked him off to hospital. Among the other French pilots, Lt Chaput crashed and was injured, while the ace of aces, Guynemer, was wounded and hospitalized. Nungesser, Fonck and Jean Navarre fought on, but it was an increasingly grim business.

One day in July, Nungesser made a lone diving attack on six German scouts over Houthulst Forest. He made a single pass, shooting down two of them and then using his superior speed to get away. The others made off eastwards under the command of a young pilot who, after flying two-seater reconnaissance missions with a unit known as *Abteilung* 5, had recently transferred to single-seaters with *Jasta* 27. His name was Hermann Göring.

When the ground offensive began on 31 July much of the Allied effort was switched to attacks on enemy airfields and infantry columns with light bombs as well as machine guns. For the first time in the war, large-scale ground attack operations were carried out by the fighter units, with devastating effect on the closely-packed enemy troops and supply columns. However, it was dangerous work, and casualties from ground fire were heavy. Moreover, the terrain was highly unfavourable for a forced landing. 'In front of us,' wrote René Fonck, 'there was nothing but miles and miles of spongy ground, where water crept stealthily into the tiniest hole. The whole area was a vast quagmire that could swallow up an object as big as a tank without trace.'

By September 1917, the Allied fighter squadrons in Flanders had succeeded, for the time being, in establishing a measure of air superiority. On 25 September, the RFC's fighters claimed nineteen victories for the loss of only one British aircraft. No 56 Squadron, which had returned to France in July after a brief period on air defence duty in England, continued to be in the forefront of the battle; by the end of September its score of enemy aircraft destroyed had risen to two hundred. This figure was matched, on 9 October, by No 1 Squadron, now equipped with Sopwith Camels.

Then, just as the Allies were starting to gain the upper hand in the air, there came a new and alarming development that was to have an enormous bearing on the conduct of the entire war. In November 1917 the revolutionary Bolshevik regime in Russia signed an armistice with the Germans. This meant that the hundreds of thousands of German troops, together with their supporting artillery and aircraft, which had been tied down in the war with Tsarist Russia could now be released for service on the Western Front. The signs for 1918 were ominous, and the Allied leaders were well aware that the survival of their cause on the Continent depended, above all else, on how soon the Americans could get into the war.

Chapter Two

Air reconnaissance, January–March 1918

The New Year of 1918 dawned to find the Allied armies in a state not far removed from utter exhaustion. The French Army was perhaps in the worst condition, and had been in steady decline ever since its spring offensive of 1917 had petered out amid tragic and bloody loss. After that, it had scarcely been in a fit state to mount any major offensive during the remainder of the year except at Verdun, where it had registered some success in the summer; moreover, its High Command had been rocked to the foundations by widespread mutinies among its embittered soldiers. The British had suffered fearful losses in men and materiél in the bitter and protracted Third Battle of Ypres, while on the Southern Front the Italians had been utterly crushed at Caporetto. The armistice at Brest-Litovsk, although its terms had yet to be finalized – and until they were, the Germans dare not risk moving men *en masse* from the east – had dealt a bitter blow to any Allied hope of breaking the deadlock of trench warfare and of securing an early victory in 1918.

The war diaries of the time record that a strange and ominous silence hung over the snow-shrouded wasteland of Flanders during

Below: Royal Aircraft Factory RE 8.

Above: RE 8 of No 52 Squadron, showing the large four-bladed propeller.

Below: An RE 8 armed with eight 25 lb Cooper bombs.

the early days of 1918. Only in the air was there activity on any scale, and much of that involved routine reconnaissance. One of the first sorties flown by the Allies was carried out early on New Year's Day by three RE 8 reconnaissance aircraft of No 3 Squadron, Australian Flying Corps, which photographed the entire Australian Corps' front in the Messines sector; the reconnaissances showed signs of heavy transport at the rear of the German lines, and revealed that ammunition dumps were increasing and more gun positions being built, a sure sign that the enemy was planning large-scale offensive action once the weather improved.

Number 3 (Australian) Squadron, which had arrived in Flanders in September 1917, had seen some hard fighting during the previous weeks. Flying from Savy, halfway between St Pol and Arras, it was attached to No 1 (Corps) Wing RFC and ordered to act as support squadron to the RFC squadron on duty with the two Army Corps in the line: No 5 Squadron RFC, with the Canadian Corps, and No 16 Squadron RFC with XIII Corps. All three squadrons were equipped with the Royal Aircraft Factory RE 8, the most widely used British two-seater on the Western Front. It was armed with one forward-firing Vickers gun and a Lewis gun in the observer's cockpit, and its RAF 4a engine gave it a top speed of around 102 mph. It was a far from robust aircraft, and the Germans did not find it difficult to shoot down.

Nevertheless, the RE 8 – nicknamed 'Harry Tate' after the celebrated music hall comedian – could give a good account of itself, as was shown on the afternoon of 17 December 1917 when an aircraft of No 3 (Australian) Squadron, ranging for an eight-inch howitzer battery, was attacked by six Albatros DV scouts. Although hard pressed, the RE's pilot, Lt J.L.M. Sandy, shot down one Albatros; its wounded pilot made a forced landing in the Australian lines and was taken prisoner. Then another RE 8 came up and its pilot and observer joined Sandy in engaging the enemy. The two REs fought the five Albatros for nearly ten minutes, until the Germans saw a third RE approaching and broke off the engagement.

The pilot of the second RE, Lt E.J. Jones, flew close to Sandy's aircraft, which was cruising normally, and thought that its pilot and observer, Sgt H.F. Hughes, were uninjured and that they were continuing their sortie, so he flew back to base to rearm. The next day, No 3 Squadron received a telegram to say that the bodies of Sandy and Hughes had been found in their wrecked aircraft near St Pol. An examination showed that a bullet had passed through the observer and lodged in the base of the pilot's skull. The aircraft had flown itself in wide left-hand circles until it ran out of fuel, and then crashed about fifty miles south-west of the battle area. Sandy was recommended for the immediate posthumous award of the Military Cross and Hughes for the Distinguished Conduct Medal.

Another German pilot who fell victim to an RE 8 was Lt Max Müller, one of *Jasta* Boelcke's leading pilots. On 29 November 1917, Müller scored the *Jasta*'s 179th victory and then became a flight commander under the new *Staffelführer*, Lt Walter von Bülow. On 16 December he scored his thirty-eighth and final victory, shooting down a Sopwith Camel west of Passchendaele.

Von Bülow was killed on 6 January 1918, and Müller was appointed *Staffelführer* in his place. On 8 January, Müller visited the *Jagstaffelschule* at Valenciennes and delivered a lecture to a class of student pilots on the best methods of shooting down an RE 8. The next day he was back with his *Jasta* at Marke, taking off at the head of six more Albatros D Vs to put his theories into practice. Near Passchendaele, he sighted an RE 8 and led his pilots down for a formation attack. Captain G. Zimmer, the pilot of the RE 8 – which belonged to No 21 Squadron RFC, said by many to be the finest artillery observation squadron on the Western Front – saw the seven Albatros coming down on him and turned hard, enabling his observer, 2nd Lt H. Somerville, to put a good burst into the leading Albatros at close range. The Albatros, after firing one burst at the RE 8, suddenly veered away and began to glide with its engine stopped. Then it burst into flames and dropped away out of control.

A few thousand feet lower down, Max Müller jumped from the cockpit of his blazing aircraft and plummeted to his death near the ruined town of Moorslede. The other German pilots, horrified, broke off their attack on the RE 8, which escaped over the front line.

One of the more experienced RFC reconnaissance pilots was Captain John A. Pattern, who had joined No 10 Squadron at Abeele in Belgium in May 1917. Armed with BE 2es when Pattern joined it, No 10 re-equipped with Armstrong-Whitworth FK 8s later in the year. Designed by Frederick Koolhoven, the FK 8 – known as the 'Big Ack' by its crews – was used by Nos 2, 8, 10, 35 and 82 Squadrons on the Western Front at the beginning of 1918. Its 160 hp Beardmore engine gave it a top speed of around 90 mph and it carried an armament of one synchronized Vickers gun, operated by the pilot, and a Lewis gun in the rear cockpit. Although heavy on the controls, it was well built and robust, could absorb a lot of battle damage and was well liked by its crews. Major K.D.P.

Murray, No 10 Squadron's commanding officer, said of it:

> 'The big A-W was slow, but my pilots liked it for the particular job they had to do, and never regarded themselves as 'cold meat'. Owing to the nature of their work, they were rarely in a position to attack, but when attacked, as they were frequently enough, they gave a good enough account of themselves.'

John Pattern and his observer, Lt Leycester, definitely gave a good account of themselves in the course of a photographic sortie over the trenches on 29 November 1917. Pattern himself, shortly before his death – he was then in his nineties – told the story to the author.

> 'I was due to go home on leave the following day, and when you had been warned for leave you weren't supposed to fly. But after several days of fog and rain the weather had finally cleared and there were reports of large enemy troop movements south of Passchendaele, so as the Squadron's most experienced pilot I was detailed to go out and get the photographs that were urgently needed. It wasn't that I was a particularly good pilot; it was just that most of the others who had been on the Squadron when I joined it six months earlier were dead. On average, a crew doing our sort of job, flying straight and level over the enemy lines, could expect to last three weeks before being shot down. Some of us, myself included, were lucky; I had been shot down only a week before in a scrap with five Albatros D.IIIs, and my observer and I had walked out of the wreck with only a few scratches. That was one of the good points about the big A-W; it was so strongly built that crews could often walk away from the most horrendous crashes.'

On that November morning, Pattern and Leycester – it was their seventh mission together – took off from Abeele and climbed to 5,000 feet, heading towards Ypres and the front line. Unknown to them, some thirty miles away another pilot was also taking off from an airfield near Lille. He was *Leutnant* Erwin Böhme, a *Staffel* commander in the Richthofen *Jadgdgeschwader*.

This was a big day in Böhme's life. In a few hours' time he was due to receive Germany's highest award for gallantry – the *Ordre Pour le Mérite*, or 'Blue Max' as it was nicknamed – from the hands of the *Kaiser* himself. The medal was Böhme's reward for shooting down twenty-four British and French aircraft, but to him its significance was much greater. It would help to remove a burden of guilt he had carried for over a year, since October 1916.

Together with his *Staffel* commander, Oswald Boelcke – the most famous German air ace of that time – he had been involved in a dogfight with some British aircraft. Böhme had made a slight error of judgement; his wingtip had touched Boelcke's and the ace's aircraft had gone down, breaking up as it fell. Boelcke had been killed instantly. Desolate, Böhme had gone to his tent on landing and taken out his revolver, intent on committing suicide, but had been prevented by von Richthofen. Now, in November 1917, Böhme commanded Boelcke's old unit, *Jagdstaffel* 2.

Böhme headed for the front line, accompanied by five more Albatros Scouts, intent on claiming one more victim before he received his decoration. The victim shoud have been John Pattern, whose FK 8 was crossing the front line just north of Westhoek. Pattern takes up the story:

> 'About a quarter of a mile on the enemy side of the lines, I turned south-east and Leycester started to work his camera. The anti-aircraft fire, which had been intense, had stopped, but I didn't take much notice. I should have known better; it was a sure sign that enemy fighters were in the vicinity. Suddenly, I heard the clatter of Leycester's machine-gun above the roar of the engine. I looked round to see what he was shooting at, and nearly had a heart attack. Slanting down from above,

Above: The Armstrong-Whitworth FK 8 gave excellent service and could absorb tremendous punishment.

getting nicely into position thirty yards behind my tail, was an Albatros.

'I immediately heaved the old A-W round in a split-arse turn, tighter I think than I had ever turned before. I felt a flash of panic as I lost sight of the Hun, but Leycester must have been able to see him all right as he kept on firing. My sudden turn had done the trick. The Albatros overshot and suddenly appeared right in front of me. Because of the relative motion of our two aircraft, he seemed to hang motionless, suspended in mid-air. I could see the pilot's face as he looked back at me.

'I sent a two-second burst of Vickers fire into him. His aircraft seemed to flutter, then slid out of sight below my starboard wing. I was pretty certain that I had hit his petrol tank. Behind me, Leycester was still blazing away. He was using tracer, and it may have been one of his bullets that ignited the petrol pouring from the Hun's ruptured tank. When I caught sight of the Albatros again, it was burning like a torch and side-slipping towards the ground, trailing a streamer of smoke. For an instant I saw the German pilot, looking down over the side of the cockpit. Then the smoke and flames enveloped him.

'I pushed the A-W's nose down and headed flat out for home, aware that the other Hun scouts were coming down after me. They would probably have got me, too, if some friendly fighters had not come along just in time and driven them away. To say that I was relieved would be the understatement of the century.'

The first week of 1918 found Capt Pattern attached to No 21 Squadron at La Lovie, flying RE 8s in the Passchendaele sector, and his log book records a 'scrap with seven enemy aircraft' on 4 January. He returned to No 10 Squadron on 9 January, the usual activity of trench reconnaissance being broken by an occasional sortie to direct an artillery shoot. The weather was bad, and several sorties were flown in snow and strong winds. Number 10 Squadron was now carrying out night bombing attacks in addition to reconnaissance, and it was on one of these that Pattern's luck finally deserted him. The targets were the railway stations at Menin and Courtrai, and Pattern – flying alone – was bracketed by anti-aircraft fire as he crossed the front line on his way home. Severely concussed and knocked senseless, he regained consciousness to find himself flying upside down, perilously close to the ground. He recalled righting the aircraft, and had no recollection of anything else until he found himself within sight of a light beacon which he recognized as Abeele's. He turned in to land, but hit some trees on the approach and crashed.

After several weeks in hospital, John Pattern resumed flying duties at the end of May 1918, instructing on DH 6 primary trainers at No 11 Training Depot Station, Old Sarum, Wiltshire. He never returned to the front.

While Pattern lay in hospital, the German Chief of Staff, 53-year-old General Erich Ludendorff, had been putting the finishing touches to his master plan: the great spring offensive that would drive a wedge between the Allied armies and throw the British into the sea. After much wrangling the armistice terms with the Bolsheviks had at last been thrashed out, making it possible for the transfer of divisions and supporting equipment to the Western Front.

Ludendorff, aware that this would be his last chance of securing a major victory before the powerful resources of the United States were thrown into the war in France, knew that his marginal superiority of 200 divisions against the Allies' 175 would not be enough to sustain an offensive in more than one sector of the front. The whole plan depended on a single swift hammer-blow; the problem lay in selecting the spot on which the full weight of the blow was to fall. Some of Ludendorff's staff officers advocated striking against the French, but Ludendorff objected; he pointed out that if the French were defeated the British would almost certainly go on fighting, but if the British were defeated the French would probably give in. Besides, the French were more manoeuvrable than the British, experienced in fluid rather than static warfare; it might prove hard to effect a complete breakthrough in their sectors. There was no doubt in Ludendorff's mind that the blow must be directed against the British.

As February gave way to March, the German divisions that were to take part in the attack swung forward to their jumping-off positions. Seldom, since the early months of the war, had the morale of the German troops been so high. As the time of the attack approached, officers and men were fully briefed on what was expected of them, so that there was no room for rumour or doubt. So thoroughly had all the preparations been made that failure was regarded as an impossibility. If the attack should be held up at any one point, operations were to cease there immediately and the troops switched to another sector.

Four army groups were deployed between Arras and La Fère. The most northerly was known as the Mars Group; this was detailed to meet and parry any counter-attack from the direction of Arras, so protecting the flank of the first main attacking army. This was the 17th Army under General Otto von Below; code-named Michael I, it was to be launched against Crosilles and Bullecourt. By mid-March, the strength of the German Flying Corps operating in support of the 17th Army had virtually doubled to include seventeen reconnaissance *Staffeln*, seven *Schlachtstaffeln* (ground attack squadrons), thirteen *Jagdstaffeln* and three bomber *Staffeln*. These units were deployed on thirty-one airfields in the Lille area.

Immediately south of Michael I was the 2nd Army under General von der Marwitz, code-named Michael II; this was directed against Bapaume and Péronne. In support of the 2nd Army were sixteen reconnaissance *Staffeln*, eleven *Schlachtstaffel*n, ten *Jagdstaffeln* and three bomber *Staffeln*, deployed on thirty-three airfields in the area to the east of Cambrai and St Quentin.

Finally, in the area around St Quentin itself, was the 18th Army (Michael III) under General Oskar von Hutier, its strength substantially bolstered by the speedy transfer of the reserve divisions of the Crown Prince of Prussia from the Champagne Front north-east of Chalons. The 18th Army was supported by sixteen reconnaissance *Staffeln*, nine *Schlachtstaffeln*, twelve *Jagdstaffeln* and six bomber *Staffeln*. Its task was to drive a wedge between the French and British armies; the latter would then be encircled and destroyed by the two northern German army groups.

The number of *Staffeln* engaged in support of a

Below: A Rumpler C IV, one of the most effective German observation aircraft, in flight over the Western Front.

Below: Rumpler C VII pictured after a landing mishap. The C VII could reach a ceiling of nearly 24,000 feet in 50 minutes.

particular army would fluctuate somewhat as the offensive developed, and air units were switched from one sector to another as required. By the third week of March, the Germans had air superiority on the Somme, with 730 aircraft, including 326 fighters, opposing 579 Royal Flying Corps machines, of which 261 were fighters. Opposite the French sectors the Germans had a further 367 aircraft of all types; the French *Aviation Militaire*, as it was now known, had some 2,000 military aircraft of all types in service at this time, but no accurate figure exists for the numbers deployed in any given sector.

The Germans employed two principal types of photographic reconnaissance aircraft on the Western Front early in 1918: the Rumpler C VII and the Halberstadt C III. The Rumpler was the better of the two in most respects and came in two versions, one designed for long-range reconnaissance and carrying wireless telegraphy equipment and the other carrying additional photographic equipment and oxygen apparatus for the two crew, who were also provided with electrically heated flying suits. Service ceiling of the C VII, which was armed with either one or two machine guns, was nearly 24,000 feet, which it could reach in about fifty minutes, and at that altitude it could outrun any Allied fighter type, even if the Allies had possessed one capable of climbing so high. Neither Britain nor France had a reconnaissance aircraft in the Rumpler C VII's class, and the aircraft ranged more or less at will over the Allied side of the lines in the period before the spring offensive, gathering photographic intelligence that was to prove invaluable to Ludendorff's planners.

Above: A Halberstadt C III two-seater. This example belonged to the Austro-Hungarian Air Corps.

Chapter Three
Strategic bombing, 1917–18

During the winter of 1917–18, while the RFC's observation crews battled their way through increasingly foul weather to bring back information on the progressive German buildup, strenuous efforts were being made at home to reorganize Britain's air defences. The day of the large-scale Zeppelin raids on Britain was over, hampered by the weather and lack of navigational aids from the beginning, and finally crippled by the growing proficiency of the RFC's night fighter crews and the anti-aircraft defences. But from the summer of 1917 a much greater threat emerged with the beginning of sustained attacks by the Gotha bombers of *Kagohl* 3 (the unit's designation being an abbreviation of *Kampfgeschwader der Obersten Heeresleitung*, or High Command Bomber Wing).

Powered by a pair of 260 hp Mercedes D IV liquid-cooled in-line engines, the Gotha G IV could carry a typical war load of six 110 lb bombs. Its maximum speed was about 85 mph, which even so was faster than some of the fighter aircraft sent up to intercept it, and its attack altitude of 16,000 feet made it a difficult target, unless defensive fighters had ample warning of its approach. The first attack on the British mainland, mounted by twenty-three Gothas in daylight on 25 May 1917, killed 95 civilians and injured 195 in Folkestone. More than seventy home defence aircraft were sent up to intercept, but the only ones to make contact

Below: Gotha G IV bombers of *Kagohl* 3 at Gontrode.

Above: Gotha bombers pictured over Essex on their way home after attacking London on 7 July 1917.

Above: The mightiest German bomber of WWI: The *Staaken* R VIII Giant and the men needed to handle it, in the air and on the ground.

were flown by two ferry pilots. Several Gothas were destroyed in subsequent raids, but these mostly fell to anti-aircraft fire or failed to regain their base because of adverse weather. The few home defence aircraft that did get close enough to intercept were usually beaten off by the Gotha's substantial defensive armament of three Spandau machine-guns.

In September 1917 the Gothas switched to night attacks, and they were now joined by an even more formidable bomber: the Zeppelin (*Staaken*) R Type, known as the *Riesenflugzeug* (giant aircraft). This monster was capable of carrying a 2,200 lb bomb load at 14,000 feet at 80 mph under the power of its four 260 hp Mercedes engines; moreover, it was defended by five machine-guns, which made it a much tougher target than the Gotha. Only a small number of R Types were built, but they presented an immense threat to British targets.

To meet this threat, the War Office implemented a new defence scheme whereby anti-aircraft guns and patrolling aircraft were allocated separate operating zones. In addition, balloons trailing steel cable 'curtains' floated in barriers up to 8,000 feet, theoretically forcing any attacking aircraft to fly above that height to a level where fighters would be patrolling. Sound locators – simple trumpet devices at first, followed by more sophisticated fixed sound mirrors – were also playing their part by the end of 1917; the first sound mirror, a fifteen-foot reflector cut into the chalk cliff at Fan Bay, east of Dover, and focused on a point midway between Dunkirk and Calais, was operational by October 1917, and was able to detect aircraft sounds at up to fifteen miles.

The first German bombing raid of 1918 was mounted on the night of 28/29 January, when thirteen Gothas and two Giants were despatched to attack London. In the event seven Gothas and one Giant succeeded in doing so, killing 67 civilians, injuring another 166, and causing damage of nearly £190,000. The raid was thwarted to some degree by fog, as far as the Gothas were concerned, while one of the Giants had engine trouble and was forced to turn back, having jettisoned its bombs into the sea off Ostende.

Crossing the English coast at intervals from 8.00 pm between Harwich and the North Foreland, three Gothas bombed London and the remaining four attacked Ramsgate, Margate, Sheerness and Sandwich. The Giant also reached

Above: Gotha G III.

London just after midnight, and one of its 660 lb bombs caused the worst single bombing incident of the war when it hit the Odhams Press building in Long Acre, killing 38 people and injuring 85.

One of the Gothas involved in the London attack, crewed by *Leutnant* Friedrich von Thomsen (navigator and commander), *Feldwebel* Karl Ziegler (pilot) and Walther Heiden, dropped its bombs on Hampstead at 9.45 pm and was then tracked by searchlights as it flew over north-east London. The beams attracted the attention of two patrolling Sopwith Camel pilots of No 44 Squadron from Hainault – Captain George Hackwill and Lt Charles Banks – who at once gave chase and independently picked up the glow from the Gotha's exhausts as it passed over Romford at 10,000 feet. Banks was flying a Camel with an unconventional armament; in addition to its normal pair of Vickers guns it also carried a Lewis, mounted on the upper wing centre section and using the new RTS ammunition. Designed by Richard Threlfall and Son, this combined explosive and incendiary qualities.

It was Banks who attacked first, closing from the left to about thirty yards behind the Gotha and opening fire with all three guns. Hackwill meanwhile closed in from the right and also opened fire, effectively boxing in the German bomber and presenting an impossible situation to its gunner, whose field of fire was restricted. After ten minutes or so the Gotha caught fire and dived into the ground near Wickford, where it exploded. It would almost certainly have crashed anyway, even if it had not caught fire, for a subsequent examination of the crew's bodies revealed that the pilot had been shot through the neck. Hackwill and Banks were each awarded the Military Cross for their exploit. Other Gothas were also attacked that night, briefly and without result, by pilots of Nos 39, 50, 61 and 78 Squadrons RFC, and by a Sopwith 1½-Strutter of the RNAS from Dover.

An hour after the last Gotha had cleared the coast, the *Riesenflugzeug* was over Sudbury, having made landfall over Hollesley Bay, east of

Ipswich, and was droning towards London via a somewhat tortuous route. By this time, at least forty-four fighters were searching for it. It was sighted by two of them, from an unidentified squadron, not long after crossing the coast, but they lost contact with it and it was next sighted by the crew of a No 39 Squadron Bristol Fighter at about 11.00 pm near Harlow. The pilot of the Bristol, Lt John Goodyear, positioned himself behind the Giant and fired a long burst from his Vickers, but was then hurled aside by the slipstream; this Giant, an R 12, was fitted with six coupled engines driving three propellers, and the wash they created was enormous.

He tried again, and the same thing happened. On the third attempt, with the Bristol now running through heavy defensive fire, he attempted to position underneath the Giant so that his gunner, 1st Air Mechanic W.T. Merchant, could bring fire from his Lewis gun to bear. At that moment a burst of fire from one of the German gunners shattered the Bristol's petrol tank and wounded Merchant slightly in the arm. A few moments later the engine stopped and Goodyear glided down to make a faultless engine-off landing at North Weald, whose flare-path he had seen in the distance.

Shortly after it had released its bombs over London, the Giant was picked up east of Woolwich by a Sopwith Camel of No 44 Squadron flown by Lt Bob Hall, a South African. Hall followed it as far as Foulness, cursing in helpless frustration all the way because he could not get his guns to work. The Giant got away.

The anti-aircraft barrage scored one success that night, but unfortunately its victim was a Camel of No 78 Squadron flown by Lt Idris Davies, whose engine was stopped by a near shell burst at 11,000 feet over Woolwich. Davies tried to glide back to Sutton's Farm, but he hit telegraph wires near the Hornchurch signal box and was catapulted out of the cockpit. He fell between the railway lines, amazingly without injury, but the Camel was a complete loss. Forty minutes later Davies was sitting in another Camel, ready to take off if need be. Mostly, the anti-aircraft gunners co-operated very well with the RFC, and held their fire when friendly fighters were known to be overhead. The following night witnessed the most remarkable night battle of the war, when three Giants out of four despatched attacked southern England. The fourth, having developed engine trouble over the Channel, bombed fortifications near Gravelines before returning to its base, while the other crossed the English coast between Southend and the Naze. One of these, the R 26, developed engine trouble soon after crossing the coast and began losing height, so its crew jettisoned the bomb load and limped back across the Channel on two engines, eventually landing at Ostende.

A second Giant, the R 39, came inland via the Blackwater estuary just after 10.00 pm, and ten minutes later it was sighted by Captain Arthur Dennis of No 37 Squadron, who was flying a BE 12b. The latter, developed from the older BE 2c, had enjoyed some success in the night fighting role, one of No 37 Squadron's aircraft having shot down Zeppelin L48 in June 1917. It was armed with a single Lewis gun, mounted on the port side of the cockpit and synchronised to fire through the propeller. Dennis opened fire from close range, braving fire from two of the Giant's machine-guns, and scored hits on the bomber's fuselage before drawing off to change his ammunition drum. On the second approach, however, he was buffeted by the giant's slipstream, and on recovery found that he had lost contact with the target.

The R 39 approached London from the north-west at approximately 11,000 feet and was next sighted by Bob Hall of No 44 Squadron, who pursued it until it became lost in the haze near Roehampton. Once again, Hall's guns gave trouble and he had no opportunity to open fire. Meanwhile, the Giant had dropped its bombs on residential areas between Acton and Richmond

Above: Sopwith Camel flown by Major G.W. Murlis Green, DSO, MC, of No 44 Squadron – one of the leading home defence night fighter pilots – taking off from Hainault Farm, Essex.

Park, the crew having apparently mistaken Hammersmith Bridge for Tower Bridge, which was several miles to the east. South of the Thames, the R 39 was attacked briefly and with no visible result by Capt F.L. Luxmoore of No 78 Squadron, flying a Sopwith Camel. He fired fifty rounds on his first pass, but as he made a second firing run one of his bullets struck the Camel's propeller and the brilliant tracer element flew back into his face, temporarily blinding him. By the time his night vision was restored, the bomber had vanished.

Shortly after this the R 39, now down to 9,500 feet and travelling very fast, was located by Capt. G.H. Hackwill of No 44 Squadron, who was also flying a Camel. Hackwill gave chase and fired 600 rounds from long range before shortage of fuel compelled him to break off. The Giant was last seen as it crossed the coast near Hythe by 2nd Lts F.V. Bryant and V.H. Newton, the crew of an Armstrong-Whitworth FK 8 of No 50 Squadron. They too gave chase, but lost the bomber in haze.

The third Giant, the R 25, crossed the coast near Foulness at 10.50 pm and was almost immediately attacked by 2nd Lt F.R. Kitton of No 37 Squadron, flying a BE 2e. Diving his aircraft at a shuddering 100 mph, he got under the Giant's tail and fired a complete drum of ammunition at it, observing several hits, but lost the bomber while he was busy rearming. The R 25 was next attacked by Bob Hall of No 44 Squadron at 11.15 pm over Benfleet, but his guns kept jamming as he pursued it. He was joined by 2nd Lt H.A. Edwardes, also of No 44 Squadron, who fired

Below: FE 2b of No 51 (Home Defence) Squadron, Tydd St Mary, Lincolnshire. The FE was hopelessly out-performed by the bombers it was supposed to catch, and could not climb fast enough to intercept a Zeppelin.

three long bursts before his guns also jammed.

By this time the R 25 was taking violent evasive action. The battle had now attracted three more Camels, all from No 44 Squadron; the first on the scene was 2nd Lt T.M. O'Neill, who fired 300 rounds before his guns jammed too. Next came the squadron commander, Major Murlis Green, who was flying a Camel equipped with two Lewis guns using RTS ammunition. He had already made one run, only to break away when he almost flew into O'Neill's fire. Now he closed in again to be greeted by the full attention of the Giant's rear gunner. Undeterred, he fired threequarters of a drum at the bomber before suffering a stoppage which he was unable to clear. As his second Lewis also refused to function, he had no choice but to return to base to have the trouble put right.

The R 25 was now in trouble. The Camels' fire had put one of its engines out of action and some of its instruments had also been smashed. Although unable to maintain height with a full bomb load, and with their speed down to about 60 mph, the crew decided to press on to London. The Giant's bombs fell in open ground near Wanstead. Up to this point the R 25 had been harried by Bob Hall, who was able to fire only five rounds before each stoppage; he now lost his target, but encountered the R 39 a few miles to the west.

The R 25 scraped home to Ostende, having survived successive attacks by five fighters. They had collectively fired over 800 rounds at her, and after landing she was found to have taken no fewer than eighty-eight hits. Had the fighters not suffered continual gun stoppages, there seems little doubt that they would have brought down the bomber. However, there were other factors in their failure to do so; analysing the action later, the Camel pilots of No 44 Squadron realized that the Giant's sheer size had led them to believe that they had been firing from a much closer range than was actually the case. Instead of closing to within fifty yards, as

Above: One that didn't make it: a Friedrichshafen G III bomber shot down in France.

they had thought at the time, they must have been anything up to 250 yards away.

There was no doubt that the Germans were a long way ahead of anyone else, in terms of equipment and practical application, in the strategic bombing field at the beginning of 1918; but the British, once they had begun to develop the concept, were not slow in catching up. During the early weeks of 1918, the Air Staff in London had been giving considerable thought to the expansion of an RFC bombing force to undertake long-range attacks on industrial targets and communications inside Germany. Such a force already existed in embryo; in September 1917 the 41st Wing RFC, comprising three squadrons under the command of Lt-Col C.L.N. Newall, had been formed specifically to undertake attacks on German targets in response to the Gotha raids on the British mainland. Of the three units, No 55 Squadron was equipped with Airco DH 4s for the day bombing role, while Nos 100 (FE 2b) and 16 (Handley Page O/100) Squadrons were reserved for night bombing.

The 41st Wing's first attack was carried out on 17 October 1917 by No 55 Squadron against the large steelworks at Saarbrucken-Burbach. Eleven DH 4s took off from Ochey and eight of them attacked the target, killing four people, injuring four and causing 17,500 marks' worth of damage. On 21 October the same squadron sent out twelve DH 4s to bomb factories and railway yards at Bous, on the Moselle north of Hangendingen and about sixty miles from the squadron's base. One aircraft turned back with engine trouble, but the remainder pressed on and bombed the objective from 15,000 feet. On the way home from the target the DH 4s were attacked by ten Albatros Scouts but managed to beat them off, claiming four enemy aircraft destroyed for the loss of one DH 4, whose pilot, Captain Daniel Owen, succeeded in landing behind the German lines despite being severely wounded in the left eye.

This operation highlighted the excellent qualities of the DH 4, a highly versatile aircraft which, to the RFC, was in many ways what Geoffrey de Havilland's Mosquito was to be to the RAF in the Second World War. Powered by a 160 hp Rolls-Royce III or V engine, it had a top speed of 117 mph, an endurance of three and a half hours and a good defensive armament of one fixed forward-firing Vickers gun and one or two Lewis guns in the rear cockpit. Its maximum war load was two 230 lb or four 112 lb bombs, or an equivalent weight of smaller weapons.

Above: Airco DH 4s of No 5 (Naval) Squadron at Petite Synthe, about to take off on a sortie.

Above: Airco DH 4s.

Above: Handley Page O/100, the 'Bloody Paralyzer', flanked by a Nieuport Scout and Sopwith Triplane.

Designed from the outset for high speed bombing, the DH 4 was far more effective than the FE 2b, which had originated as a fighter. The FE had fought well against the Fokker Monoplane in the summer of 1916, but it had soon become outclassed by a new generation of German fighters such as the Albatros and had been introduced to the night bombing role. Its 120 hp Beardmore engine gave it a top speed of barely 80 mph. As it was a 'pusher' type, its observer sat in the extreme nose, operating a forward-firing Lewis gun and a second Lewis on a telescopic mounting over the wing centre section firing upwards and rearwards. It could carry one 230 lb or three 112 lb bombs. The cockpit layout provided excellent visibility when conditions were good, but in the winter the crew often had difficulty in locating their targets because they were blinded by rain or sleet. Sometimes, they arrived back at base so stiff and numb with cold that they had to be lifted from their cockpits. Despite its drawbacks, however, the FE 2b was to continue in service with No 100 Squadron until August 1918.

The 41st Wing's third bomber type, the Handley Page O/100 – which equipped No 16 (Naval) Squadron – owed its origins to a requirement, issued in December 1914, for a 'bloody paralyser of an aeroplane' for the bombing of Germany. The nickname subsequently bestowed upon it by its crews was inevitable, but the 'bloody paralyser' adequately met, and in some cases exceeded, its requirements in the role it was intended to perform. Powered by two Rolls-Royce Eagle II engines, it had a speed of around 75 mph and carried a four-man crew, with positions for single or twin Lewis machine-guns in nose and dorsal locations and another Lewis firing downward and rearward through a trap in the floor. It could carry sixteen 112 lb bombs or eight 250 lb bombs internally, two and half times the load it had been designed to lift. The O/100 had entered service with No 3 Wing RNAS on the Western Front in November 1916, and from the spring of the following year its two squadrons, Nos 14 and 16, had concentrated on the night bombing of major German installations such as U-boat bases, railway stations and industrial centres. Consequently, when No 16 Squadron was detached to form part of the 41st Wing in September, it brought considerable experience with it.

The first operation of the 41st Wing's night bombers was flown on 24 October 1917, when, on a squally, blustery night, nine O/100s and sixteen FE 2bs took off from Ochey, the Handley Pages to attack the Burbach works and the FEs to bomb railway yards between Falkenburg and Saarbrucken. Number 16 Squadron failed to locate the target and two of the O/100s failed to return, but No 100 Squadron's FEs reported several direct hits on their objective, including one on a train by a 230 lb bomb.

During its first month of operations the 41st Wing carried out eight raids and dropped over eleven tons of bombs, but with the onset of bad weather in November only five more raids could be undertaken before the end of the year. There was no doubt by this time that the enemy regarded the 41st Wing's efforts as more than just a nuisance, for they bombed Ochey twice in November and twice in December. During the night attack on 4/5 December, they damaged sixteen of the Wing's aircraft.

Sporadic raids on German targets resumed in January 1918, but because of the weather and various other factors these were mostly short-range affairs. On 1 February the status of the 41st Wing was upgraded and it was redesignated VIII Brigade, Newall being promoted to the rank of brigadier-general. At the same time, work began on getting three new night bomber and three day bomber airfields ready for operations.

On 18/19 February No 100 Squadron flew its longest-range mission so far, sending eleven FEs out to attack Trier, a round trip of 200 miles. Some of the aircraft flew so low over the town that the German anti-aircraft gunners were compelled to cease fire for fear of their shells causing more damage to Trier than the raiders' bombs. The next day it was the turn of No 55 Squadron, which despatched ten DH 4s under Capt. J.B. Fox to Mannheim, with Kaiserlautern as an alternative target. The mission got away to a bad start when one of the DH 4s got out of control in a cloud and went into a spin; the pilot recovered at 1,000 feet and returned to base, severely shaken and in an overstressed aircraft. A second aircraft lost contact with the rest of the formation and it also returned. Over no-man's land, the other DH 4s ran into a very strong and unexpected headwind that cut down their ground speed so much that it soon became obvious that they would not reach either of their selected targets. They therefore bombed Pirmasens, between Saarbrucken and Karlsruhe, which was the principal production centre of German army boots. All the attacking aircraft returned safely to Ochey, having encountered no opposition from either anti-aircraft fire or fighters.

Chapter Four
Skirmishes, January–March 1918

At the beginning of December 1917, *Groupe de Combat* 12 (GC.12), with its two fighter *escadrilles* – SPA.3 *Cigognes* and SPA.103 – parted company with the Flanders front and flew to Maisonneuve in the Aisne sector. From there, they carried out a number of escort missions with observation aircraft attached to General Duchene's Sixth Army. However, increasingly bad weather made air operations virtually impossible, and GC.12 was ordered up to Beauze-sur-Aire in the Argonne, the move being completed by 19 January; there, the group was attached to General Hirschauer's Second Army, holding the sector west of Verdun.

Groupe de Combat 12 was now commanded by *Commandant* Hormant, who had replaced Brocard. On the day of the group's return, Hormant proposed an offensive patrol over enemy territory; René Fonck, *Capitaine* Pierre d'Harcourt and another pilot, Lt Fontaine, volunteered, all of them from SPA.103. Over the front line they encountered a superior formation of enemy aircraft, which they attacked. In the middle of the fight, Fonck noticed that Fontaine was in difficulty, his engine having apparently failed, and was being harassed by two German machines. Fonck quickly shot down his own adversary, then dived on Fontaine's attackers. Within seconds one of them, too, was spinning down in flames. The other fled and Fontaine made a safe emergency landing.

On 27 January, taking advantage of a break in the increasingly poor weather, Lt Georges Madon of SPA.38 shot down his twenty-first victim, and two days later destroyed a two-seater which had strayed too far inside French

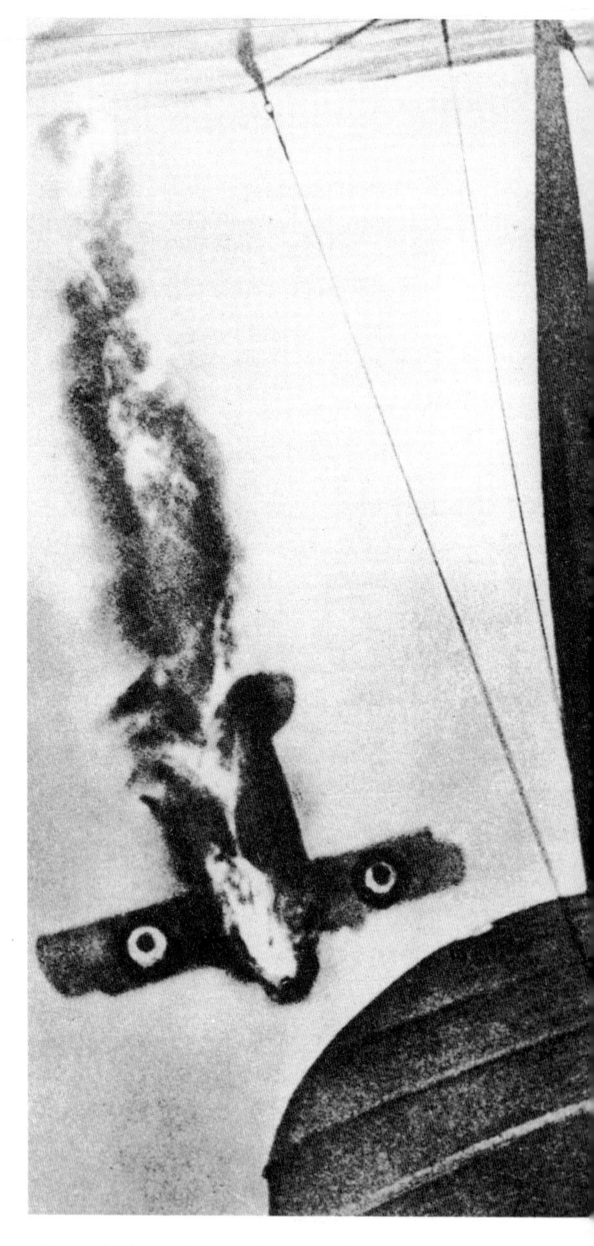

Above: Although heavily retouched, this photograph is nevertheless genuine. It shows what appears to be a Nieuport 27 falling in flames.

Above: The Nieuport 24 was the first Nieuport fighter to feature a circular-section fuselage.

Below: The Nieuport 27 was used by No 29 Squadron RFC until replaced by the SE 5 in April 1918.

territory for its own safety. Another was destroyed by Charles Nungesser. On 3 February Madon shot down two more, bringing his score to twenty-four, and destroyed another a few days later after a hectic fight with six enemy scouts. Nungesser, still in top place, was working hard to gain his thirty-second victory, but so far success was eluding him. Among the talented fighter pilots of the *groupes de combat*, the race to be 'ace of aces' was on again.

In the Verdun sector, René Fonck of SPA.103 had a curious encounter in the third week of February 1918 with a German two-seater nicknamed *Fantomas* by the French. The aircraft was an LVG with distinctive markings – the nature of which is unfortunately unrecorded – and during the winter of 1917–18 its unnamed crew had become notorious for their highly accurate trench strafing attacks. In November 1917 a French pilot named René Montrion claimed to have shot the troublesome LVG down, but it cropped up again shortly afterwards and continued to put in frequent appearances, despite subsequent claims to its destruction. Then, one cold February morning, René Fonck caught the LVG as it was approaching the French lines, doubtless intent on yet another strafing run. This time there was no mistake, and the burning remains of *Fantomas* were scattered over no–man's land.

Above: Bristol F 2B C4814 of No 11 Squadron.

On the Flanders front, too, flying operations were severely hampered by foul weather in the first weeks of 1918, but on the few favourable flying days there were some spirited combats between the opposing sides, the RFC crews often finding themselves outnumbered. Most of the activity took place in the second half of the month, and the following extracts from the operations record of No 43 Squadron – then based at La Gorgue under the command of Major C.C. Miles – are fairly representative of fighter operations during this period.

17 February. Trollope's patrol of five Camels encountered an enemy formation of eight machines. As a result of the combat which ensued three enemy machines were driven down out of control.
18 February. Captain Trollope while on a special mission (alone) saw three Armstrong-Whitworths under attack by six enemy machines. He at once attacked the enemy who were then joined by six more. Trollope fought the twelve for ten minutes until all his ammunition was exhausted, by which time the enemy machines had all flown away to the east.
19 February. Second Lieutenant R.J. Owen whilst on patrol on his own was attacked by five enemy scouts in the vicinity of the Bois de Biez. He fought the five, one of which according to the testimony of anti-aircraft gunners was seen to fall in flames.
26 February. Captain Trollope leading a patrol of nine Camels saw four DFWs escorted by fifteen enemy scouts. He led the patrol into the attack. Although gun trouble prevented him from joining in he stayed in the middle of the fight and saw two enemy machines crash and a third fall out of control.

At the beginning of March, there were plenty of indications that the expected German offensive in Flanders was not far away. Despite

Above: Sopwith Camels of No 210 Squadron RAF. The nearest aircraft, B6289, was flown by the Canadian ace W.M. Alexander. The pilots of the next two aircraft were Lts F.V. Hall and D.L. Nelson.

continuing bad weather the enemy's air effort intensified, with much activity by observation aircraft. There were some brisk engagements, and on 12 March the Richthofen *Geschwader* engaged nine Bristol Fighters of No 62 Squadron, which was operating north of Arras as part of the 9th Wing, and destroyed four of them. The next day, farther south in 13th Wing's sector, seven Camels of No 43 Squadron, escorting a pair of FK 8s, encountered a mixed force of fifteen Albatros and Pfalz Scouts and attacked them; Captain Henry Woollett fired at one, which broke up in mid-air, then engaged a second, which went out of control and crashed. Two more were shot down by 2nd Lt Peiler, and one each by 2nd Lts Lingham, Lomax, King and Dean. A ninth enemy aircraft was shot down by an observer in one of the FK 8s, which belonged to No 2 Squadron, whereupon the remainder broke off the action and flew away.

On 16 March, seven Camels of No 4 (Australian) Squadron, which was part of the 10th (Army) Wing, took off from Bruay to attack targets near Douai with 20 lb bombs. The attack was carried out without incident, but as the Camels were climbing to 16,000 feet to cross the front line they were hotly engaged by a formation of sixteen brightly-painted Albatros Scouts, readily identifiable as belonging to the Richthofen *Geschwader*. While four of the Albatros remained at altitude, ready to dive down and pick off stragglers, the other twelve attacked in pairs.

The Australian flight commander, Lt G.F. Malley, and Lt C.M. Feez avoided the first pass and went in pursuit of the two Albatros, which were diving in formation. The Australians shot both of them down. Meanwhile, Lt A.W. Adams, some 2,000 feet lower down, fought a hectic battle with two more scouts and destroyed one of them, while Lt W.H. Nicholls, pursued down to ground level, was forced to land behind the German lines and was taken prisoner. Another Camel pilot, Lt P.K. Schafer, was attacked by three Albatros of the high flight; as he was attempting to evade, the Camel flicked into a spin and fell 10,000 feet before the shaken Australian managed to recover. He landed at Bruay with sixty-two bullet holes in his aircraft.

On the following day, Captain John Trollope of No 43 Squadron sighted six enemy scouts while flying alone on an altitude test (a favourite ploy of pilots lacking the necessary authorization to carry out lone patrols over the front line). He climbed above them and attacked, sending one down out of control. The other five dived away. Shortly afterwards, while returning to base, Trollope sighted four more enemy aircraft and attacked one of them at close range. It caught fire and broke up. Trollope at once turned to engage the rest, but they flew away eastwards.

On 18 March, a German NCO pilot, forced down and captured, admitted under interrogation that the offensive would begin on 20 or 21 March. On the evening of the 20th, RFC observation aircraft, taking advantage of a break in the weather, returned with intelligence that enemy troops in the front line were being relieved by fresh units, a sure sign that an attack was about to develop. The warnings were not ignored; all along the front, the Allied forces were placed on full alert.

Above: Sopwith Camel.

At nightfall on 20 March 1918, the Order of Battle of the Royal Flying Corps on the Western Front, under the command of Major-General J.M. Salmond, was as follows:

IX (GHQ) Brigade: (Brig-Gen Hogg)

Ninth Wing: Lt-Col Freeman

Sqn	CO	Aircraft	Base
25	Duffus	DH 4	Villers-Brettoneux
27	Hill	DH 4	Villers-Brettoneux
62	Smith	Bristol F 2B	Cachy
73	Hubbard	Camel	Champien
79	Noel	Dolphin	Beauvais
80	Bell	Camel	Champien

54th Wing (Night Bombing): Lt-Col Small

Sqn	CO	Aircraft	Base
58	Tyssen	FE 2b	Clairmarais
83	Gower	FE 2b	Auchel

I Brigade (Brig-Gen Pitcher)

First (Corps) Wing: Lt-Col Gossage

Sqn	CO	Aircraft	Base
2	Snow	FK 8	Hesdigneul
4	Saul	RE 8	Choques
5	Gardner	RE 8	Ascq
16 (Can)	Portal	RE 8	Complan l'Abbé

Tenth (Army) Wing: Lt-Col Maclean

Sqn	CO	Aircraft	Base
3 (Naval)	Collishaw	Camel	Treizennes
4 (Aus)	McLaughty	Camel	Bruay
8 (Naval)	Draper	Camel	Teteghem
10 (Naval)	Bell	Camel	Treizennes
18	Howard	DH 4	Treizennes
40	Dallas	SE 5a	Bruay

II Brigade (Brig-Gen Becke)

Second (Corps) Wing: Lt-Col Blake

Sqn	CO	Aircraft	Base
3 (Aus)	Brown	RE 8	Bailleul
7	Sutton	RE 8	Moreuil
9	Rodwell	RE 8	Proven
10	Murray	FK 8	Abeele
21	Gould, L.T.N.	RE 8	La Lovie

Eleventh (Army) Wing: Lt-Col van Ryneveld

1	Barton Adams	SE 5a	St Omer
6	MacLaren	DH 9	Bertangles
9 (Naval)	Butler	Camel	Clairmarais
19	Pretyman	Dolphin	Bailleul
20	Johnston	Bristol F 2B	St Marie Cappel
29	Dixon	Nieuport 17	La Lovie
32	Russell	SE 5a	Bailleul
57	Hiatt	DH 4	St Marie Cappel
60	Moore	SE 5a	Filescamp
65	Cunningham	Camel	Poperinghe

Thirteenth (Army) Wing: Lt-Col Playfair

3	Barker	Camel	Warloy Baillon
11	Morton	Bristol F 2B	La Bellevue
22	McKelvie	Bristol F 2B	Treizennes
41	Bowman	SE 5a	Lealvilliers
43	Miles	Camel	La Gorgue
46	Mealing	Camel	Filescamp
49	Gould, J.R.	DH 4	La Bellevue
56	Brown	SE 5a	Baizieux
64	Smythies	SE 5a	Izel-le-Hameau
70	Edwards	Camel	Marieux
102	Baker	FE 2b	Izel-le-Hameau

III Brigade (Maj-Gen Higgens)

Twelfth (Corps) Wing: Lt-Col Mitchell

12	de Courcy	RE 8	Boiry St Martin
13	Garrod	RE 8	Etrun
15	Stammers	RE 8	Lechelle
59	Mackay	RE 8	Courcelles-le-Comte

V Brigade (Brig-Gen Charlton)

Fifteenth (Corps) Wing: Lt-Col I.A.E. Edwards

8	Leigh-Mallory	FK 8	Templeux
35	Holt	FK 8	Estrée -en-Chaussée
52	Morison	RE 8	Bonneuil
53	Henderson	RE 8	Villeseneux
82	Jackson	FK 8	Bonneuil

Below: SPAD VII of No 23 Squadron RAF. The type also equipped No 19 Squadron.

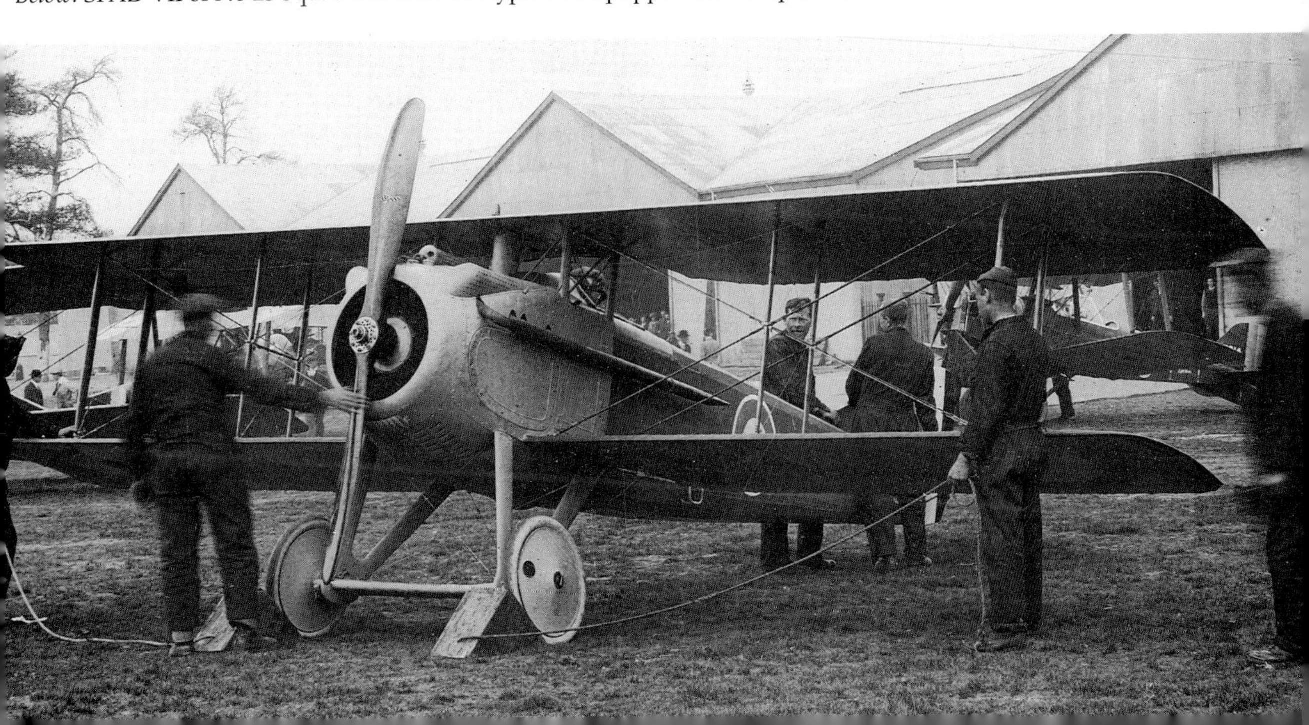

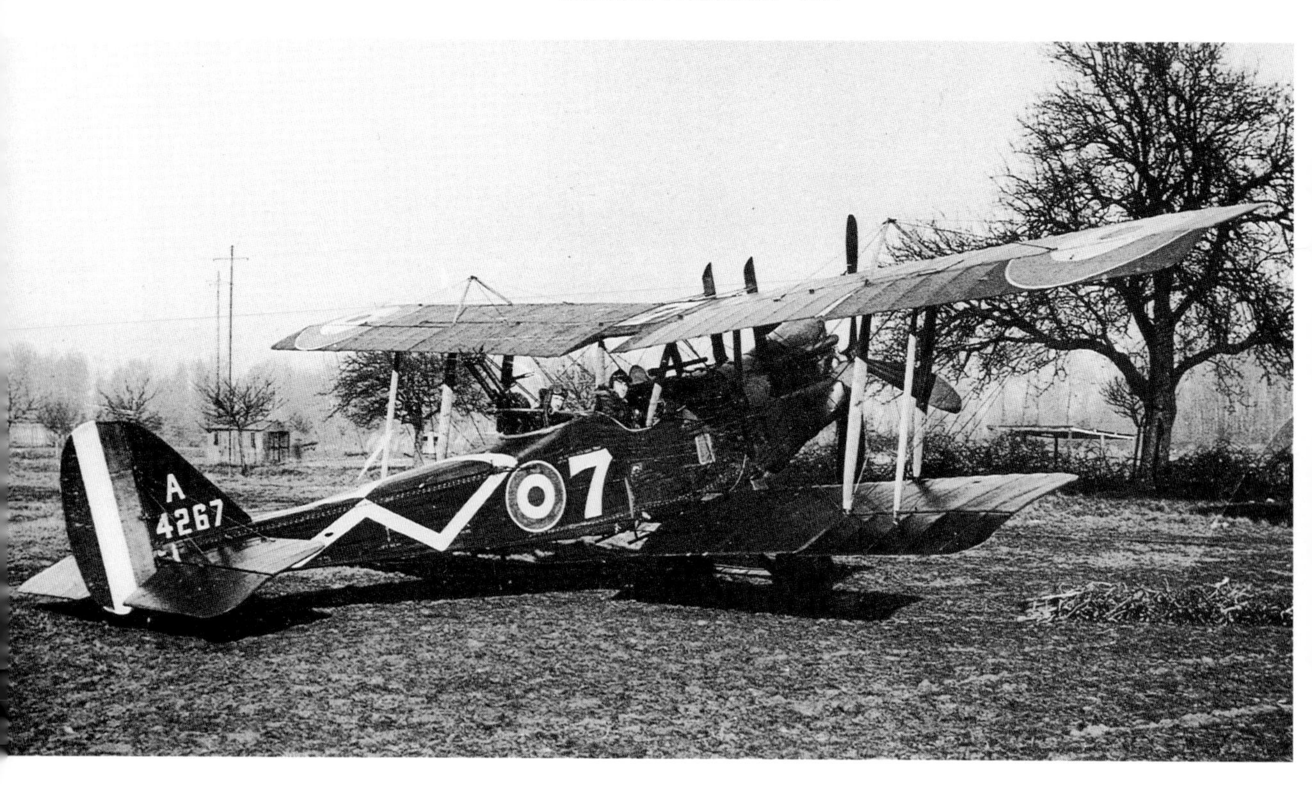

Above: RE 8 of No 52 Squadron, showing the unit's distinctive markings.

Twenty-Second (Army) Wing: Lt-Col Holt

5 (Naval)	Goble	DH 4	Bois de Roche
23	Bryant	SPAD XIII	Matigny
24	Robeson	SE 5a	Matigny
48	Shield	F 2B	Flez
54	Maxwell	Camel	Flez
84	Douglas	SE 5a	Flez
101	Hargrave	FE 2b	Catigny

Of these formations, the RFC's III Brigade had the task of supporting the Third Army (General Byng), which on 20 March had eight divisions in the line and seven in reserve, while the Fifth Army (General Gough), with eleven divisions in the line and three infantry and three cavalry divisions in reserve, was supported by V Brigade. It was on these two British armies that the weight of Ludendorff's offensive would fall. At 4.45 am on 21 March, 1918, the German artillery opened up with a furious barrage of high explosive and gas shells that pounded the whole length of the British-held front. More than fifty miles of the front, from Monchy to Tergnier, was flooded with poison gas. Long-range artillery was also brought into action, shelling supply dumps and communications centres up to twenty-eight miles to the rear. The German observation aircraft had done their work well; all known or suspected British gun positions had been meticulously plotted and were now attacked with the aim of weakening the defensive shell curtain and counter-battery fire, and all ground likely to be sheltering reserves was heavily shelled. Then, out of the dense mist, advancing behind a creeping barrage of high explosive, fifty-six German divisions hurled themselves forward to the attack.

Chapter Five
'All risks to be taken.'

General Gough's Fifth Army, outnumbered by four to one, was soon reduced to isolated units, pockets of resistance making gallant last stands far behind the forward German echelons, their surviving artillery fighting close-range actions over open sights. For several vital hours neither the men in the forward positions, nor the staff officers at Brigade, Division, Corps and even Army Headquarters had any real idea what was happening. Communications had been severed by the preliminary artillery onslaught; frantic light signals went unobserved in the fog, which also rendered air reconnaissance impossible on Fifth Army's disintegrating front. On the left, General Byng, commanding the Third Army, had slightly better intelligence, thanks to the crew of a solitary RE 8 of No 59 Squadron, which took off into the murk as the sun was rising and, flying at almost ground level, was able to monitor the German advance for more than an hour before it was hit and put out of action by a shell.

About mid-morning, the mist thinned sufficiently to allow more reconnaissance sorties to be flown. There followed a stream of signals from excited RFC crews, indicating a profusion of targets ranging from sunken roads clogged with masses of German infantry to gun batteries being brought into action or moving forward. For the first time, air observation revealed the extent of the disaster that had befallen the two British armies. Every available RFC aircraft that was capable of attacking targets on the ground was thrown into the fray, but operations were hampered throughout 21 March by continual adverse weather, which was worst in Fifth Army's area. All day long, the aircrews flew through shifting veils of fog and mist that would part briefly for a few seconds to reveal enemy forces pushing relentlessly across country from St Quentin. The squadrons co-operating with the Fifth Army attacked wherever and whenever they were able, while the Corps squadrons did their best to provide the British artillery with worthwhile targets.

That they failed to do so led to a great deal of unfair criticism of the squadrons involved. But as historian Hilary St George Saunders pointed out in his book *Per Ardua*:

> 'The reasons why the Corps squadrons on this and on succeeding days had so little success was very simple. In the storm and stress of battle, the organization for securing a full and effective measure of co-operation between the pilots in the air and the gun crews on the battery sites broke down. When the battle and the war were over this deficiency provided much food for the arguments of many and thoughts of a few . . . The Royal Flying Corps, it was said, had let slip a wonderful opportunity; well-directed artillery fire might have so disconcerted the enemy as to have thrown his attack into confusion or even halted it. The critics, both civilian and Service, forgot, or did not choose to remember, one vital factor. Communication from the air to the ground was maintained by wireless and to receive messages it was necessary to erect an aerial. This was what the artillery only too often failed to do. It is not fair to blame them, any more than it is fair to blame the RFC. Batteries had to shift their positions, very often several times a day, and sometimes several times an hour. In such circumstances they could not, or at least did not,

erect their wireless masts. Even when, in rare instances, they did so, the battery commander, more often than not, not only did not know the zone calls but was also ignorant of the zone which the battery was supposed to cover. One instance will suffice to make this dreadful situation clear. On the night of 21st-22nd March, T. Leigh-Mallory, the officer commanding No 8 Squadron, sent his wireless officer to do all that he could with such spare equipment as was available to help the wireless operators attached to the batteries with which he was trying to co-operate. The officer made a tour of them and found not one mast erected or in action. In the haste and confusion of the retreat, most of the batteries had abandoned their wireless equipment. "As soon as the retreat had started," runs his report, "all idea of co-operating with aeroplanes seems to have been abandoned."'

In the Third Army's sector, air observation by another 59 Squadron RE 8 (Capt D.H. Oliver and 2nd Lt W.H. Leighton) was able to report by 3.50 pm that a deep bulge had been made in the British lines between Bullecourt and Doignies, placing the left flank of the Fifth Army in jeopardy.

To add to the RFC's problems, many of the British forward airfields were now within range of enemy artillery, and some were even in danger of being overrun by German troops. For example, Major Goble's No 5 (Naval) Squadron, which had just moved up to Mons-en-Chausée with its DH 4s, was very quickly shelled out of it again, forcing a move back to Bois de Roche. By nightfall on 22 March, seventeen squadrons had been compelled to evacuate their aerodromes and move back to safer locations, having first destroyed anything that might be of use to the enemy.

The German Flying Corps moved up quickly to occupy the abandoned airfields. In the words of one account (*Die Deutschen Luftstreitkrafte im Weltkriege*, G.P Neumann):

'After the first front line had been broken through, we advanced rapidly. As the closest possible touch had to be kept with the infantry, it was essential that they should be followed by aeroplanes, and only by such means was it possible to transmit orders and messages, for the despatch riders and runners, owing to the rapidity with which we advanced, were not able to carry out the heavy work imposed upon them.

'In order to preserve the integrity of the various flying units, their transfer to aerodromes in the devastated area was effected by groups in convoys of lorries. Aerodromes were first reconnoitred by a photographic machine, and were then divided up among the groups, so that each group was self-contained in its own sector. Special aerodromes were provided for the fighting machines, and on the third day of the attack the enemy's aerodromes which had been closest to the line were used by us. Practically all material found on these aerodromes had been destroyed by fire.'

Confused and sporadic air operations continued throughout the 22nd. A patrol of No 2 (Australian) Squadron on this day was perhaps typical of many experiences along the battlefront.

'Ten SE 5as set out to patrol St Quentin; two had to turn back with engine trouble, but the other eight encountered five enemy two-seaters escorted by a number of single-seaters. Lieutenant Forrest dived on a two-seater, which burst into flames, and Lieutenant McKenzie sent an Albatros down out of control. Turning north along the front, the Australians passed over Bourlon Wood, where they spotted five German Triplanes below. Captain Phillips attacked the leader, who rolled over and went into a slow spin; the other Triplanes scattered in the haze. Over Bullecourt more Albatros Scouts were engaged; Lieutenant Forrest shot down two out of control and Lieutenant Holden got a third.'

On 23 March, as the weather began to clear a little, Allied observation aircraft brought back more information on the enemy's movements and the scale of his penetration, enabling the General Staff to plan counter-moves. Now, for the first time, the RFC found itself in a position to influence the course of the battle. A magnificent defence by the British infantry divisions in the centre of the Third Army's sector, south-east of Arras, kept the line intact, but the right flank near Bapaume was hard-pressed and fighting a desperate rearguard action as the troops strove to maintain contact with the fragmented and retreating Fifth Army. It was in this sector, on the 23rd, that some of the most intensive air operations took place.

The Camels of No 4 (Australian) Squadron were in the thick of the fighting here. On the morning of the 23rd, the Squadron received orders to attack the Germans near Vaux-Vraucourt and along the Bapaume–Cambrai road. Two flight of six Camels took off just after 10.00 am, led by Captain Courtney, and flew to their objective at low level, keeping under 500 feet the whole way. The low-level attack took the enemy troops by surprise, the bombing and strafing throwing the Germans into confusion and panic. Top cover during the initial attack was provided by Lt G.F. Malley's six Camels, which dived on several Albatros attempting to attack the strafing flight. Malley shot down two of the enemy fighters, and 2nd Lt Scott destroyed a third.

Bapaume was now in enemy hands, and later in the day No 4 Squadron was ordered to attack British ammunition dumps there which had not been destroyed by the retreating troops. Whether the dumps were hit or not is not recorded, but the Camels were attacked by enemy fighters soon after dropping their bombs. One Australian pilot, Lt A.E. Robertson, shot down one Fokker Triplane and 'drove two others down out of control'.

The strafing attacks were already beginning to have an effect on the Germans, as the war diary of the 73rd Regiment, describing events of 22 March, reveals.

'The English got valuable support from their aircraft which attacked regardless of consequences. The squadrons, flying very low, found profitable targets for bomb and machine-gun in the thickly concentrated masses of the 111th Regiment . . . about a dozen English low-flying aircraft whizzing up and from an incredibly low height bombed our advancing troops. This caused great confusion . . . '

The following day, Sunday 24 March, was critical. Some fighter squadrons, which had been operating from bases outside the immediate battle area, were now moved closer to it in order to provide escort for the all-important ground attack and observation aircraft, and to establish the air superiority that was so vital to the RFC's effort. One of them was No 43 Squadron, which moved from La Gorgue, near Merville, to Avesnes-le-Comte near Arras.

On the first patrol of 24 March, Captain John Trollope, leading a flight of Camels, sighted three DFW two-seaters and worked his way round to the east to cut off their line of escape. He closed in and fired at the first, but then his guns jammed. After clearing the stoppage he engaged the second DFW and fired 100 rounds at it, seeing it break up in mid-air; he at once closed on a third and set it on fire. Meanwhile, the first DFW had been engaged by Capt. Cecil King and 2nd Lt A.P. Owen, who continued to fire at it until it too broke up. Some Albatros Scouts arrived belatedly to protect the DFWs, and Trollope immediately shot one down. At a lower level, another flight of 43 Squadron Camels led by Captain Henry Woollett was engaging more DFWs, one of which Woollett set on fire. Lieutenant Daniel of Woollet's flight, losing contact during the engagement, joined up with No 3 (Naval) Squadron, which attacked five Pfalz Scouts. Daniel destroyed one of them, bringing 43 Squadron's score on that patrol to seven.

That afternoon Trollope led a second patrol into action, despite deteriorating weather condi-

Above: Sopwith Camels of No 3 (Naval) Squadron preparing to leave Mont St Eloi, March 1918.

tions. Soon after crossing the front line he sighted four enemy two-seaters attacking a pair of RE 8s; five or six German single-seat fighters were also in the vicinity. Trollope led his pilots down to the aid of the REs and he singled out one of the two-seaters, firing in short bursts as he closed in to almost point-blank range. He saw pieces fly off the enemy aircraft's wing, and then the whole wing collapsed. Turning hard, Trollope came round for a stern attack on another two-seater, running through heavy defensive fire from the German observer as he did so. A few moments later the German was dead in his cockpit and the aircraft spiralling down in flames. Almost at once, Trollope engaged a third two-seater which was flying at very low level; after a short burst of fire the enemy aircraft nose-dived into the ground, disintegrating on impact.

Pulling up, Trollope saw one of the squadron's Camels hard pressed by a dozen German scouts, so he climbed hard to assist, soon joined by 2nd Lts Owen and Highton. He saw each of these pilots destroy an enemy aircraft and engaged one himself, but then his ammunition ran out and he was forced to break off.

In the afternoon, nine Camels led by Henry Woollett fired 6,800 rounds in strafing attacks on enemy troops, and Woollett also shot down two observation balloons. By the end of the day, Lt 'Bert' Hull, No 43 Squadron's records officer, could report to his CO, Major Miles, that the unit had broken all previous records, having destroyed twenty-two enemy aircraft without loss in the day's fighting, and that the destruction of six by Captain Trollope in a single day had created a new RFC/RNAS record.

On this day, too, the war diaries of the German units involved in the offensive bore witness to the growing effectiveness of the air onslaught to which they were being subjected. The diary of the 100th Grenadier Regiment stated that: 'Early in the day the First and Second 100th were ordered to assemble near Athies and suffered losses of eight officers and 125 men in a few seconds from air bombs.'

The war record of the 8th Grenadier Regiment was even more descriptive.

> 'As we were moving forward after crossing the Somme, there suddenly appeared before us some twenty British aeroplanes which dived to a height of about 100 metres and then, continuing to two or three metres off the ground, attacked us with their machine-guns. Several Tommies flew so low that their wheels touched the ground. My company commander, Lt Nocke, had to fling himself flat, but for all that, he was struck on the back by the wheels of one machine, thus being literally run over. Not far from me an aeroplane appeared at about one metre from the ground making straight for me and for the moment I did not know in what direction to throw myself; the pilot appeared determined to run over me.'

Air attacks by the SE 5s of Nos 24 and 84 Squadrons, and the SPADs of No 23 Squadron, dropping 25 lb bombs, also prompted the comment that the Second Bavarian Regiment had suffered 'considerable losses . . . The Signals Officer, the excellent Weisz, was killed outright. The regimental staff was decimated.'

The next day, 25 March, was also a time of crisis. At 7.30 am, the crew of a No 59 Squadron

RE 8 reported very large concentrations of enemy infantry just east of Bapaume and requested heavy artillery fire, but the call remained unanswered, presumably because no one was there to receive it. By this time, part of the area covered by the right flank of the British Fifth Army had been taken over by units of the French Third Army, hastily thrown into the battle, but they too came under very heavy pressure and were relentlessly driven back. By the afternoon, the whole Allied line was crumbling.

It was time for desperate measures. With the Germans sweeping on in the north through Ervillers, in the centre to the outskirts of Thiepval and Montauban down to the Somme at Ham, and in the south towards Hattencourt, Champien and Noyon, Amiens itself – the main British supply and communications base – must surely fall if the enemy drive were not to be checked quickly. Early that afternoon, after consulting with the Chief of the Air Staff, Sir Hugh Trenchard, the C-in-C of the RFC in France, Major-General Salmond, issued a dramatic directive to the commander of IX (GHQ) Brigade, which had not yet been fully committed to the battle but held as a reserve force.

> 'I wish you,' [Salmond said,] 'as soon as you can after receipt of this, to send out your Scout squadrons on to the line Grevilliers–Martinpuich–Maricourt. These squadrons will bomb and shoot up everything they can see on the enemy's side of the line. Very low flying is essential, all risks to be taken. Urgent.'

The Brigade's 9th Wing, comprising Nos 25 and 27 Squadrons (DH 4), No 62 Squadron (Bristol Fighter), Nos 73 and 80 Squadrons (Camel) and No 79 Squadron (Dolphin)

Below: SE 5a of No 29 Squadron, April 1918.

responded magnificently, flying as long as the light lasted, bombing and strafing the enemy columns, flying back to base to rearm and then returning to repeat the process. Hitherto, most of the bombing and strafing had been directed against the Germans' infantry reserves, and this new assault on their communications routes left them severely shaken, as the diarist of the 52nd Reserve Regiment admitted:

> 'Enemy airmen, flying low, delay the march with machine-gun fire and bombs . . . hostile airmen are present in droves. We count more than thirty above us at any one time . . . Airmen came down to twenty metres in order to release their bombs. One Grenadier regiment has suffered such casualties that it has had to be relieved.'

Above: Sopwith Dolphin of No 79 Squadron.

The battle was also joined by squadrons of I Brigade's 10th (Army) Wing, which at this time included two Sopwith Camel units: Major McLaughty's No 4 Squadron, Australian Flying Corps, and No 3 Squadron RNAS, which was commanded by Major Raymond Collishaw. 'Collie', as he was predictably nicknamed, was a Canadian from Nanaimo, British Columbia, and had been a member of the support team which had accompanied Captain R.F. Scott's ill-fated Antarctic expedition of 1912. On the outbreak of war two years later, at the age of twenty-one, he had abandoned his career as a seaman and volunteered for flying duties with the RNAS.

Collishaw had gone first to France flying a Sopwith Pup on escort missions. Changing to Sopwith 1½-Strutters, he scored his first victory on 12 October 1916, shooting down a Fokker Monoplane near Oberndorf. Two weeks later he destroyed two more enemy aircraft in a single sortie, an exploit that earned him the French *Croix de Guerre*. Because of the promise he showed as a pilot and fighter leader, he was allowed to form a Canadian flight of No 10 RNAS Squadron, then equipped with Sopwith Triplanes. He had always been impressed by the distinctive markings adopted by many German fighter pilots, so he had the flight's Triplanes doped black all over and bestowed names on them: *Black Death, Black Roger, Black Sheep, Black Prince* and *Black Maria*, the latter his personal aircraft.

The 'Black Flight' quickly became renowned along the front, its five pilots achieving respectable scores, often in combat with the Richthofen *Geschwader*. In June 1917 one of them, Lt J.E. Nash from Hamilton, Ontario, was shot down and killed by the German ace Karl Allmenröder, who in turn was shot down and killed by Collishaw on the 25th of that month. By the time Collishaw was sent home to Canada for a rest in July, his personal score stood at thirty-seven enemy aircraft.

Returning to the Western Front in November, Collishaw was appointed CO of No 13 Squadron RNAS, one of the units responsible for the defence of Dunkirk, and he shot down three more enemy aircraft on 1 December. He assumed command of No 3 Squadron RNAS shortly after Christmas, but since squadron commanders were forbidden to fly on operations for a time he had no further opportunity to add to his score, and it was June 1918 before he was able to resume operational flying.

At the time of the Ludendorff offensive the

Above: Sopwith 1½ Strutters of No 5 Wing RNAS at Coudekerque.

10th Wing also had one SE 5a squadron, No 40. This, too, was led by a distinguished pilot and commander, Major Roderic Dallas, an Australian. Dallas had also started his war as an RNAS pilot in 1915, flying Nieuport Scouts with No 1 Squadron, and had become something of a celebrity the following May by shooting down a pair of twin-engined Friedrichshafen bombers in the Dunkirk sector. By the end of the year the squadron had exchanged its Nieuports for Sopwith Triplanes, and in 1917, now under Dallas's leadership, had fought with considerable success against the élite German *Jagdgeschwader*, including Richthofen's. At the end of 1917 Dallas was rested; by this time he had scored twenty-six confirmed victories. Returning to the Western Front after a spell on home defence duties, he was given command of No 40 Squadron, and at once found himself in the thick of the fighting.

In implementation of Salmond's directive, the usual tactics employed by the ground-attack squadrons involved cratering the roads with bombs, after which the pilots would strafe the German transport as it tried to circumvent the holes. The pilots were aided in their task by the fact that the ground on either side of the approach roads was wet and boggy, causing fearful congestion. The troops could and did scatter, but regimental horse transport drawing stores, field kitchens, heavy machine-guns, mortars and reserves of ammunition had to stand under fire. Young pilots, from the English shires and the Dominions alike, openly admitted to weeping in their cockpits on the flight home from the battle area, their minds harrowed by the vision of the carnage their bombs and bullets had wrought among the luckless animals.

Losses from ground fire – mostly small-arms – were heavy, and most aircraft returned to base with battle damage. The German Flying Corps attempted to disrupt the attacks on numerous occasions, but were usually engaged and beaten off by the Allied fighters. On 25 March, for example, a flight of six Camels of No 4 (Australian) Squadron was attacked by a mixed formation of enemy aircraft as it was completing a strafing attack; two Fokker Triplanes and an Albatros were shot down by Lt A.E. Robertson, while another pilot destroyed a two-seater. The Australian squadron lost two pilots that day, one of whom was taken prisoner, and three more were wounded, all the casualties being caused by ground fire.

At night, the offensive against the enemy supply lines was continued by the FE 2bs of Nos 101, 102 and 83 Squadrons, the latter having arrived at St Omer from England on 6 March and moved up to Auchel the next day. The crews flew through storms of hail and snow in bitter cold to bomb road and rail junctions at Péronne, Bapaume and other locations.

By 26 March the pressure on the Third Army lifted, thanks to the continued air attacks and to extremely stubborn resistance by the British troops, and in this sector the immediate crisis was over; but the Fifth Army, with orders to hold the approaches to Amiens at all costs, was in desperate straits. Its only reserves were 2,200 men drawn from all manner of units, many of them non-combatant, commanded by an artillery officer who had been on his way back from leave when the German attack developed. The RFC squadrons supporting the battered remnants of the Fifth Army fought magnificently from dawn to dusk in the ground-attack role, and after dark the bombing campaign was intensified. That night, two flights of No 58 Squadron (FE 2bs) made twenty-five sorties and flew a total of fifty hours, a record that stood until the end of the war, while Nos 101 and 102 Squadrons were

Below: Major Roderic Dallas in his SE 5. Note the distinctive camouflage pattern, similar to that adopted at the beginning of WW2.

Above: FE 2bs. After its day as a fighter was over, the FE was widely used as a night bomber.

continually in action against Ham and Cambrai. Over 500 25 lb bombs were dropped on these targets in a seven-hour period, direct hits being obtained on a train, a canal bridge and transport columns.

In a dispatch to the *Daily Telegraph* the next day, war correspondent Philip Gibbs, close to the front line, wrote:

'The enemy's massed troops were here without shelter or cover of any kind, stretched on earth and sleeping if they could in the tearing cold wind. This bombardment of ours must have kept them awake, unless they were drunk with sleep, and many men must have been killed as they lay still under the high white moon. At the same time our flying raiders went out, flew very low, so that their wings were loud above the heads of the German bivouacs, and dropped bombs into their masses and spilt machine gun fire over them, and knew by the turmoil and cries that they were hurting and demoralizing the enemy. The Germans retaliated in their own way by bombing open towns full of civilians, and I was in one of them last night, not far from the lines now, when these night bombers came over and dropped their engines of death. I have never seen such moonlight in March . . . there seemed something devilish and cruel in that white light. Quite early in the evening bombs began to fall, and all about took cover, under shadows of old doorways. Raiders came over all through the night. This was in Amiens, under the great shadow of that cathedral which in the moonlight looked as insubstantial as a dream, with all its pinnacles and buttresses as white as snow . . .'

This day, 27 March, witnessed one of the bravest exploits to emerge from the air war on the Western Front. That morning, 2nd Lt Alan McLeod, a Canadian pilot flying Armstrong-Whitworth FK 8s with No 2 Squadron RFC, took off to bomb enemy transport south of Arras, with 2nd Lt A.W. Hammond as his observer. As they were beginning their attack, they were bounced by eight enemy scouts, almost certainly from Richthofen's *Jagdgeschwader* 1. In the ensuing battle McLeod positioned the FK 8 with great skill, enabling Hammond to shoot down three of the enemy fighters as they pressed home their attacks. However, the 'Big Ack' was heavily damaged in the fight and both officers repeatedly wounded. The floor of the rear cockpit was shot through and collapsed, the same burst of fire hitting the petrol tank and setting it ablaze. Despite his wounds – he had been hit five times by now – McLeod managed to clamber out of his burning cockpit to stand precariously on the lower wing. Clinging to the edge of the cockpit with one hand, he kept hold of the control column with the other, although flames were licking fiercely around it, and side-slipped the aircraft so that the slipstream took the fire away from himself and Hammond, who was still firing from what was left of the rear cockpit.

McLeod succeeded in bringing the Armstrong-Whitworth down to a heavy landing in no-man's land. By now Hammond had been hit six times and was helpless, and despite his own severe wounds and the fact that the wreck of the aircraft was coming under machine-gun fire from German troops, McLeod dragged him clear and into cover just as the aircraft's bombs began to explode amid the flames. McLeod then collapsed from loss of blood. Luckily, the plight of the two officers had been seen by some British soldiers, who braved the enemy fire to bring them both to safety. McLeod was later awarded the Victoria Cross while lying gravely ill in hospital.

Hammond recovered from his wounds and received a Bar to his Military Cross. Sadly, McLeod was less fortunate; a few months later, still weak and ill, he succumbed to the influenza epidemic that swept across Europe at the war's end.

That night, flying in stormy weather, RFC and RNAS aircraft followed up the day's air attacks by dropping 840 bombs on the enemy and firing 18,000 rounds of ammunition. But the German drive continued, and on 28 March a major assault was made on Arras. The approaching enemy columns were seen by RFC observation aircraft, however, and the attack was broken up by further bombing and strafing and some highly effective artillery support. Farther south the exhausted Fifth Army was still under heavy pressure, but observation aircraft reported particularly dense columns of enemy infantry and, in the words of the war diary of No 52 Squadron – flying RE 8s from Abbeville – 'our machines had a field day attacking columns in fours. Heavy casualties were inflicted on several enemy battalions.'

The Camels of No 43 Squadron were again airborne on the 28th, seeking out enemy reconnaissance aircraft. They found two DFWs and attacked them, but were themselves attacked by eight enemy scouts. Cecil King shot one down, but was wounded and had to break away. When the squadron got back, it was to find that Captain Trollope was missing, together with 2nd Lts Adams, Maasdorp, Prier and Owen.

John Trollope, in fact, had been hit in the hand by a bullet, crash-landed in the German lines and been taken prisoner. German doctors amputated his hand above the wrist. A sick man, he was repatriated towards the end of June, arriving home soon after the award of a Bar to his Military Cross had been announced in recognition of his exploit of 24 March. The six aircraft he had destroyed on that day brought his total to sixteen. He was just twenty years old. Later, his arm had to be amputated at the shoulder, but despite his infirmity he built a successful career for himself in civilian life. During the Second World War he applied to rejoin the Royal Air Force, was accepted and took up an administrative post with Maintenance Command.

Above: A logical development of the Nieuport 17, the Nieuport 24 was used mainly as a fighter trainer by the *Aviation Militaire*.

Although the battle was far from over, it was now clear that the German attack was beginning to lose its impetus. On the southern flank of the bulge created by the enemy advance, fresh divisions of the French Army were coming into the line to stand shoulder to shoulder with the original British forces between Noyon and Roye, and with them, from the Champagne sector, came vital support in the shape of the *Aviation Militaire*. Among the units allocated to the fighting in Picardy were the *Cigognes* – the name now encompassed both *Escadrilles* of GC.12, SPA.3 and SPA.103 – and GC.19, the latter now under the Command of Captain Albert Deullin.

René Fonck wrote later:

'All day long, the air was filled with the roar of engines. We flew so low that we almost touched the enemy's bayonets, watching the compact masses of troops wilt away before our machine-gun fire. The chaos was terrible. Panic-stricken horses charged in all directions, trampling soldiers underfoot.'

On 29 March, René Fonck, flying from Raray, the *Cigognes*' base near the river Oise, destroyed two more enemy aircraft. This brought his score to thirty-two, placing him one ahead of his rival, Charles Nungesser. Fonck appeared to have taken little pleasure in his new status as ace of aces; the slaughter in Picardy had brought about a profound change in him, and in his fellow pilots. Hitherto, war had been an impersonal affair for the most part; a burst of gunfire, a flash of flame streaking back from a stricken aircraft, a ribbon of smoke that marked its end. Somehow, the man in the cockpit had always seemed unreal. Now, for the first time, the pilots were able to see the deadly effect of their bullets on human and animal flesh from a range of only feet, and they were sickened by it. The war, after March 1918, became something to be ended as quickly as possible.

Chapter Six
Royal Air Force

While the pilots and observers of the RFC and RNAS were fighting to stem the German onslaught, a wind of change was blowing which would eventually have a profound effect on their respective Services, although the effect would not immediately be apparent. In fact, the wind had begun to blow in London on 17 August 1917, when a committee presided over by Lieutenant-General Jan Smuts had presented a report on air organisation to the War Cabinet. It recommended the formation of an Air Ministry

> 'to control and administer all matters in connection with air warfare of every kind and that the new Ministry should proceed to work out the arrangements for the amalgamation of the two Services and for the legal constitution and discipline of the new Service. . . . the day may not be far off when aerial operations with their devastation of enemy lands and destruction of industrial and populous centres on a vast scale may become the principal operations of war, to which the older forms of military and naval operations may become secondary and subordinate.'

This remarkably far-sighted report resulted in the creation of an Air Ministry on 2 January 1918, although its birth was not accomplished without a considerable amount of inter-Service wrangling. On the following day the first Air Council was formed, with Lord Rothermere as the first Secretary of State for Air. The Chief of the Air Staff (CAS) was Major-General Sir Hugh Trenchard, who was succeeded as General Officer Commanding the Royal Flying Corps in France by Major-General J.M. Salmond on 18 January. The first moves had been made towards the creation of the Royal Air Force, the first independent force of its kind in the world.

> 'The weather was fine and the visibility good. A total of 23 tons of bombs were dropped by night and 17 tons by day. Enemy aircraft were active south of the Somme, and enemy two-seaters were employed in low flying and firing at our troops. Two hostile balloons were shot down, and one hostile machine was brought down in our lines by infantry, in addition to those accounted for by aerial combat.'

Such were the terse words of Royal Air Force Communique No 1, dated 1 April 1918. There was no sense of the dramatic in it; neither was there anything to indicate that the RFC and RNAS had ceased to exist, and by their amalgamation had given birth to a new Service. And for the thousands of men and women who now found themselves members of the RAF, the overnight change meant nothing at all. For the time being, it was business as usual.

For the fighter squadrons on both sides, that meant renewing their determined efforts to shoot down the opposition's ground-attack and reconnaissance aircraft. The German ground-attack aircraft, like the RAF's, were operating intensively, as Major Neumann tells:

> 'The trench-strafing machines worked indefatigably from all heights, and on every section of the battle front, directing most of their attention against the enemy's reinforcements. They specialized in attacking the narrow roads and bridges of the

Above: Fokker Dr I Triplane.

Somme, and the results of their work were seen in the evacuated region after the enemy had retreated. In co-operation with the artillery they frequently caused great confusion at such points. Throughout the whole of the offensive the infantry contact machines were working incessantly over the lines.'

One of the fiercest – and most one-sided – air battles of 1 April took place when five Fokker Triplanes attacked a No 57 Squadron DH 4, flown by Captain F. McD. Turner, during a photographic sortie. Turner's observer, 2nd Lt A. Leach, fired thirty rounds into one of the attackers at 100 yards, sending it down in flames, but things began to look hopeless when the remaining four were joined by ten more Triplanes and Albatros Scouts. Leach fired a complete drum into one of the latter, which was seen to roll over and break up in mid-air; astonishingly, for no friendly fighters appeared to be in the vicinity, the rest broke off the attack and flew away.

In another battle that raged during the day, Captain G.E.H. McElroy, an Irish flight commander with No 24 Squadron, attacked three enemy scouts in his SE 5a, closing to well within 100 yards of one before firing a burst of 100 rounds from both guns into it. Three days later, the same pilot unhesitatingly attacked seven enemy fighters which he spotted flying eastwards over the lines and shot one of them down from fifty yards' range. Then, on 7 April, McElroy attacked one of three enemy two-seaters, braving intense defensive fire to shoot it up from fifty yards; it nose-dived into the ground. Shortly afterwards, flying through broken cloud at 3,000 feet, he sighted three SEs being attacked by five Triplanes and closed in to fire twenty rounds into one of the Fokkers from point-blank range, sending it down to crash.

One of the more immediately visible signs of the RAF's formation was the renumbering of the RNAS squadrons on the Western Front; No 3 Squadron, for example, became No 203, and No 10 became No 210. It was a pilot with the latter unit, Captain R.A. Little – an Australian – who particularly distinguished himself in the April battles. On 1 April he fired 200 rounds into a Fokker Triplane, seeing its lower wing break away as it dived earthwards. On 6 April he attacked a two-seater, opening fire in short bursts from 200 yards and closing right in to twenty yards; the enemy aircraft dived into a cloud but Little caught up with it as it emerged and attacked it again, still from close range, and saw it fall in flames. The next day, Little's patrol was attacked by ten Fokker Triplanes, one of which he sent down out of control.

Two other top pilots, Henry Woollett of No 43 Squadron and Lt D.R. MacLaren of No 46, specialised in attacks on enemy balloons, whose observers had been directing accurate artillery fire. On 2 April Woollett fired sixty rounds into a balloon and sent it down in flames, the two observers jumping clear by parachute; he then attacked a second balloon which also fell in flames, but this time no one got out. By now the Germans were making desperate attempts to haul down a third balloon, but this too burst into flames after Woollett had fired about fifty rounds into it. Balloon attacks of this kind were not popular, as the sites were always heavily defended, and sometimes the balloons were not easy to shoot down. On 3 April, for example, MacLaren and another 46 Squadron pilot, 2nd Lt J.H. Smith, fired 300 rounds into one before its envelope finally collapsed and it dropped to earth.

During this period, the main activity of Richthofen's JG.1 was to provide air cover over the deep salient created by the rapid German advance, and on 6 April the 'Red Baron's' airmen hotly engaged the Camels of No 43 Squadron. As the squadron was strafing troops at Abancourt it was attacked by enemy Triplanes; the Camel pilots destroyed four of them for the loss of one of their own and so came out firmly on top, but during a second patrol three out of six Camels failed to return, and another was wrecked in a crash landing on the British side of the lines. The pilot of this

Below: LVG C V two-seater observation aircraft. This photograph was taken after the war (note the Allied types in the background).

Above and Below: Hannoveraner CL IIIa two-seater brought down by American fighters between Montfaucon and Cierges, 4 October 1918.

aircraft, Lt C.C. Banks, was strafing enemy troops after shooting down an Albatros when his petrol tank was holed and elevator controls shot away by ground fire. Despite this, he staggered on for two miles until he reached friendly territory.

Rain, drizzle and thick mist restricted air operations on both sides during the second week of April, but on the 9th, still in poor conditions, the squadrons of I Brigade RAF were airborne, attacking enemy troops and transport between Bois Grenier and La Bassée canal and providing escort for observation aircraft. The enemy's own two-seaters came in for some punishment, five being shot down during the day. The strafing attacks continued on 10 April, but because of the continuing poor weather there were few air combats; however, Lts H.L. Taylor and W.I.E. Lane of No 52 Squadron had a stiff fight with nine Fokker Triplanes, one of which was shot down out of control by the observer. Although wounded, Lane continued to engage the enemy and shot another down in flames, enabling his pilot to escape across the lines and bring the badly damaged RE down for a crash-landing.

The next day also dawned with low clouds and mist, but by the middle of the afternoon the weather had begun to clear and there was a sharp increase in air activity all along the front, particularly south of La Bassée. One of the RAF fighter units covering this sector was Major Roderic Dallas's No 40 Squadron, Dallas himself shooting down a two-seater which he attacked from a range of thirty yards. A few days later, Dallas came very close to losing his life when his aircraft was badly hit by machine-gun fire from the ground. Although wounded in both legs he managed to reach his airfield at Bruay safely, and was back in action within a fortnight.

Two other pilots of No 40 Squadron also had success on 11 April. Late in the afternoon Captain G.H. Lewis, a flight commander, sighted seven Fokker Triplanes and attacked one of them, but was forced to break off when his guns jammed. Clearing the stoppage, he resumed his patrol and encountered a solitary triplane which he engaged, using up most of his ammunition on it until it went into a slow spin and crashed near Lens. The other 40 Squadron pilot, Captain J.H. Tudhope, also engaged the formation of seven Fokkers, attacking one at very close range and putting several bursts into it. The aircraft pulled up sharply and stalled, indicating that the pilot had probably been hit, and then spun into the ground.

The former Naval squadrons, meanwhile, had been briefed to concentrate on the enemy ground-attack aircraft which were harassing Allied troops. A flight of No 203 Squadron's Camels, led by Captain Little, encountered three two-seaters and initiated an attack, but were immediately engaged by six Albatros Scouts which were providing top cover. Little and three other Camel pilots turned to face the enemy and Little destroyed one, seeing it crash near Neuve Eglise; while they kept the Albatros occupied Lts A.T. Whealy and J.A. Glen pressed home attacks on the two-seaters. Whealy shot one down near Sailly-sur-Lys and another crashed in flames after Glen had fired 500 rounds into it.

The day had proved a costly one for the German close support squadrons, which had lost eleven two-seaters. But the RAF observation aircraft had also suffered at the hands of German fighters, and the courage of the observation crews was typified by one battle in which Lts R.G. Hart and L.F. Handford of No 15 Squadron, flying a contact patrol in their RE 8, were attacked by four Pfalz Scouts. The enemy's first firing pass shot away the RE's elevator and aileron controls, leaving it virtually helpless. As a Pfalz came in to deliver the death blow Handford fired twenty rounds into it, seeing both sets of wings break away and the fuselage burst into flames, plummeting down to crash near Millencourt. In great pain from a knee wound, Handford engaged another Pfalz, firing at it until he passed out; British troops later

Above: 2nd Lt P.D. Learoyd of No 40 Squadron (on right), who participated in the destruction of a two-seater on 29 April 1918.

reported seeing the aircraft fall in flames behind the enemy lines. One of the surviving Pfalz followed the RE down to 100 feet, but broke away sharply when the RAF aircraft reached the front line. Displaying fine airmanship, Hart managed to crash-land the crippled aircraft, using only throttle and rudder. Pilot and observer were both awarded the Military Cross.

The next day, 12 April, was fine and clear throughout, with exceptional visibility, and was marked by fierce air battles along the whole front. No 43 Squadron was again in the thick of the action, and Captain Henry Woollett equalled John Trollope's earlier record by destroying six enemy aircraft in the course of the day. His combat report tells the story.

'10.30 am. I led my patrol down on to eight EA (enemy aircraft) just south-east of La Gorgue. I fired about 30 rounds into one single-seater; machine spun down and crashed just west of La Gorgue. I then dived on to another EA (a two-seater); this I saw crash just north-east of La Gorgue.

'I climbed up and got on the tail of an Albatros and after firing about 40 rounds it burst into flames, falling to pieces. I also saw another EA in flames, and also one crash which was shot down by Lt Daniel.

'5.00 pm. I led patrol down on thirteen EA just

> north of La Gorgue. I fired about 30 rounds into one EA which was going east. This turned over on its back and fell to bits. I then climbed and got on to the tail of another Albatros; after firing several bursts into him, he spun down and crash-landed north east of La Gorgue. On returning over lines I climbed up and found another EA at about 2,000 feet; this after about 20 rounds collapsed in the air and fell to bits. I saw two other EA crash, engaged by machines of my patrol.'

All through the day, aircraft of the RAF's I and II Brigades made low-level attacks on enemy forces between Wytschaete and La Bassée canal, with the fighters of IX Brigade providing top cover or engaged in offensive operations. Among the units engaged was No 74 Squadron, now based at La Lovie and commanded by Major Edward Mannock, a man very different in outlook and temperament from most of his peers. That outlook was forcibly expressed when, a few weeks after the death in action of Werner Voss, several pilots of No 56 Squadron learned that they had been awarded decorations. Among them was Arthur Rhys-Davids, who had been awarded the DSO. That night, No 56 Squadron's mess was the scene of a wild party, and Rhys-Davids was reluctantly dragged in to make a speech. In it, he praised the qualities of the German pilots, and asked his colleagues to raise their glases to the greatest adversary of all, Manfred von Richthofen.

Mannock, who was visiting from a neighbouring unit and who had no time for chivalry, set aside his glass and remained seated. When the others looked at him, he said quietly: 'I won't drink to that bastard.'

At the age of thirty, Mannock was much older than most fighter pilots. He had two infirmities, one physical, the other psychological. The physical one was a very bad left eye; the psychological one was a chip on his shoulder, the result of a hard struggle for existence during his boyhood and youth. His father had been a corporal in the British Army, and in the late nineteenth century a corporal's pay did not stretch very far. Day after day, as a child, he had watched his mother struggle to feed him, his elder brother and elder sister, while others more fortunate appeared to squander money. To help out he had been forced to leave school early, working first as a delivery boy for a grocer in Canterbury and then as a barber's assistant. In the end he became a linesman for the Post Office; it was a job he liked, and the family with whom he lodged in Wellingborough gave him much of the affection he had missed as a child. It helped to remove many of the scars of his boyhood and kept him from being too embittered. Nevertheless, 'Mick' Mannock was to remain a confirmed socialist to the end of his days, nurturing a dream that one day he and others like him would be able to change the world.

When he was twenty he had experienced a sudden urge to see the world, working his way through the Middle East and Turkey. The experience matured him, and the sights he saw led him to believe that England might not be such a bad place after all. At any rate, he was not slow to enlist when he believed war to be inevitable in 1914, joining the Medical Corps in the first instance. This, however, was a non-combatant role, and Mannock wanted to fight, so he applied for a transfer to the Royal Flying Corps, bluffing his way through the medical examinations by memorizing eye charts.

He was accepted for flying training in 1916, and was fortunate to have as his instructor a man who was already experienced in combat: Captain James McCudden. He taught Mannock all the tricks of his new trade, and the two became firm friends. It was a partnership that only death would sever.

Early in 1917 Mannock joined No 40 Squadron in France, and it was then that McCudden's teaching paid off. Mannock worked hard to improve his flying and shooting, and despite his bad eye became a better than average marksman. Unlike many of his colleagues, he approached the science of air fighting with extreme caution, preferring to skirt the fringes of his early air skirmishes rather than throw caution to the winds and dive into the middle of a fight. Some of his fellow pilots even began to hint that he might lack courage, but Mannock took no notice. He watched his more hot-headed critics go down in flames one after the other, and knew that he was right.

After two months, Mannock was satisfied with the tactics he had been striving to perfect, and now the change that came over him in action was dramatic. In the next three weeks he shot down six enemy aircraft, earning the Military Cross and rapid promotion to flight commander. Now that he could impart his skills to other pilots he really came into his own, forging a first-rate fighting team. His pilots had the utmost trust in him; he shepherded them carefully, never lost his head in action, and always ensured that the odds were right before committing himself to battle. He became a master of ambush, and before attacking an enemy he made certain that his pilots conformed to the golden rule: 'Start the attack from above, seldom on the same level, never from beneath.' He taught his men to attack from astern, if possible, hitting the enemy on the first diving pass. He also taught them the full range of aerobatics to build up confidence in handling their aircraft, at the same time stressing that aerobatics in a dogfight were pointless and dangerous. Tight turns, he said, were the only manoeuvres that paid real dividends in an air battle.

Behind the superb fighting machine that Mannock had become, however, was one overriding fear, and he was not ashamed to admit it. Before each flight he would carefully check his revolver to make sure that it was loaded and in good working order. If he caught fire in the air, one of those bullets was for himself. He had a horror of burning to death. He seemed to feel none of this horror, though, when he witnessed one of his enemies – for whom he harboured a deep and implacable loathing – met with a similar fate. He also had a somewhat macabre fascination in collecting souvenirs from the wrecks of aircraft he had shot down. These he sent off to Jim Eyles, the man with whose family he had lodged in Wellingborough.

> 'I sent the parcel off to you yesterday (he wrote to Eyles at the beginning of August 1917). Pilot's boots which belonged to a dead pilot. Goggles belonging to another. The cigarette holder and case were given to me by the captain observer of a two-seater I brought down. The piece of fabric with a number on it is from another Hun two-seater. The other little brown packet is a field dressing carried by a Hun observer for dressing wounds when in the air. I got it from a crashed bus . . . We have only lost six of our original squadron and have brought down about forty-five Huns. My total is now forty-one, although you may not believe it, and they have given me the DSO. I'm expecting the Bar at any moment, as I have brought down another eight since I was recommended for the DSO. If I have any luck, I think I may beat old Mac (McCudden). Then I shall try to oust old Richthofen . . . '

At the end of 1917, by which time he had been posted to No 74 Squadron, Mannock's score had risen to fifty-six, and he had indeed surpassed 'old Mac'. The latter levelled the score in February 1918 with the destruction of a Hannoveraner two-seater, but then he was sent back to England, where he was awarded the Victoria Cross. He was never to have an opportunity to gain further victories. After four months in England, McCudden was promoted and ordered back to France to take command of No 60 Squadron. On 9 July 1918 he crossed the Channel in his SE 5a and landed at a French aerodrome to refuel before continuing to No 60's airfield at Boffles. On take-off, his engine failed and McCudden disobeyed one of the cardinal rules of flying, a rule he had instilled over and over again into his students: if your engine fails on take-off, never turn back towards the airfield. He did so; his aircraft lost flying speed in the turn, stalled and went into a spin. Too low to recover, McCudden was killed in the crash.

With Mick Mannock in command, No 74 Squadron arrived in France on 30 March 1918 and installed itself a few days later at La Lovie, near Poperinghe, which it shared with the Camels of No 54 Squadron under Major R.S. Maxwell. Its first patrols were flown on 12 April, and on that day Mannock celebrated his return to action in fine style, as the official summary of the day's operations records:

> 'Capt E. Mannock, 74 Sqn, after one or two pilots of his patrol had engaged a hostile machine without result, fired a burst into it. It then crashed east of Carvin. He fired a long burst with both guns at 30 yards into another EA, which went down and crashed near the first machine.'

Low cloud and mist again dominated the Flanders scene during the next few days, followed by strong winds with snow and hail storms, so that very little flying was possible. In eight days the RAF squadrons claimed only eleven aircraft destroyed and lost about an equal number of their own. Not until 21 April did the weather begin to clear, and the level of air activity rose correspondingly. Captain R.A. Little of No 203 Squadron was in action again, attacking the rearmost machine of a formation of twelve Albatros Scouts which he encountered near Vieux Berquin; he watched it fall through 1,000 feet, apparently out of control, but was then himself attacked by six more scouts, which chased him through the middle of the formation he had just engaged. Little put the Camel into a spin, and just as he did so a burst of fire shot his controls away, leaving the aircraft completely unmanageable. Little sat there helpless, resigned to a violent death when the Camel hit the ground, but suddenly the spin flattened out with a jerk so severe that it broke the fuselage under the pilot's seat. Little undid his seat belt and was hurled clear when the Camel struck the ground. Stunned, but otherwise without serious injury, he came fully to his senses to find that the enemy aircraft were taking it in turns to dive down and strafe him. Enraged, he drew his revolver and exchanged shots with one Albatros that came down to thirty feet. After a few desperate minutes the enemy aircraft were driven off by rifle and machine-gun fire from the British positions close to where Little had crashed. Within a few minutes, the pilot was sitting with the troops, gratefully sipping sweet tea heavily laced with rum.

The Bristol Fighters of No 62 Squadron, which formed part of the 9th Wing, took part in the day's action. Second Lt L.M. Thompson, the gunner in an aircraft flown by Lt D.A. Savage, opened the score by shooting down an Albatros near Lille; soon afterwards the Bristol was attacked by two Pfalz and Thompson opened fire on one of them. It went into a vertical dive and broke up in the air, whereupon the other aircraft flew away. Captain T.L. Purdon and 2nd Lt P.V.G. Chambers, part of the same patrol, fired 200 rounds between them into a Fokker Triplane and saw it go into a steep spiral dive. As it pulled out it was attacked by 2nd Lt W.E. Staton, also of No 62 Squadron, who saw it crash near Estaires.

But of all the air combats that took place on 21 April 1918, one overshadowed all the others. Its outcome was to have a profound effect on the morale of the German Flying Corps, and spark off a controversy that persists to this day.

Chapter Seven

The day 'The Baron' died

Shortly after ten o'clock in the morning of 21 April, *Rittmeister Freiherr* Manfred von Richthofen walked across the grass of Cappy aerodrome, the base of his *Jagdgeschwader* 1, towards his scarlet-painted Fokker Dr.I Triplane. He had scored his eightieth victory the day before, an event celebrated by a somewhat riotous party that evening. He was looking forward to a spell of leave, which he planned to spend hunting with some friends in the Black Forest. But that was still several days away, and in the meantime, with the German air squadrons operating at full stride in support of the offensive, which had now run out of momentum, there was much work to be done. Today, von Richthofen would be leading two *Staffeln* of fighters on an offensive patrol over the front line.

By his side trotted his black labrador, Moritz. Suddenly, an air mechanic pointed a camera at the pair, intent on securing a snapshot that would be treasured in the years to come. Most pilots, German and Allied alike, considered it unlucky to be photographed just before a flight, but Richthofen laughed at such superstitions. He smiled as he turned to face the camera. It was the last photograph that would be taken of him alive.

As he was about to climb into his aircraft, another airman came up to him with a postcard he wanted to send home to his son, and asked the pilot to sign it. 'What's the matter?' asked Richthofen in jest. 'Do you think I shan't come back?'

Twenty miles away, at Bertangles aerodrome on the other side of the lines the pilots of No 209 Squadron RAF were running up the engines of their Sopwith Camels prior to take-off. In the cockpit of one of the fighters sat twenty-four-year-old, Canadian-born Captain Roy Brown. A veteran pilot with the Distinguished Service Cross and twelve combat victories, Brown presented a very different picture from von Richthofen. Battle fatigue had taken its toll and aged him beyond his years. His face was sallow, and a nerve twitched at the corner of his mouth. He lived on a diet of brandy and milk, his stomach, tortured by stress and the castor oil spewed out by the Camel's rotary engine, constantly rejecting solid food.

Above: Albatros Scouts of the Richthofen *Geschwader*.

The man Brown would shortly meet in

Above: Pilots of Manfred von Richthofen's *Jasta* 11.

combat, Manfred von Richthofen, had joined the German Flying Corps in May 1915, having spent the first months of the war in action with the 1st Regiment of *Uhlans*. During the summer of 1915 he flew as an observer on both Eastern and Western Fronts, shooting down his first enemy aircraft, a Farman two-seater, in the Champagne sector in September. Since the Farman came down in French-held territory, however, von Richthofen was unable to claim credit for it. Soon afterwards he was accepted for pilot training, going solo for the first time on 10 October 1915. The following March, having successfully completed his course – although not without difficulty, for his instructors did not rate him highly – he joined a two-seater unit in the Verdun sector, and in April shot down a Nieuport – although this, too, fell behind the French lines and could not be claimed. There were more skirmishes during the weeks that followed, but von Richthofen had yet to gain his first official victory when, in June, his squadron was transferred to the Eastern Front to carry out bombing and reconnaissance duties.

It was still there in August 1916, when the pilots received a visit from Oswald Boelcke, on his way back to France after a trip to Turkey. Boelcke, who had received orders to form a *Jagdstaffel*, was on the lookout for talent, and

Above: Fokker Dr I of *Jasta* 11

Above: Albatros D V of *Jasta* 12. Note the swastika marking: a symbol of good luck in 1918, with none of the evil connotations later attached to it.

Below: Hauptmann Hermann Göring in the cockpit of a Fokker D VII.

von Richthofen – who had met Boelcke once before, on a train – soon pushed himself forward. Despite von Richthofen's poor record at flying school, Boelcke recognized enthusiasm when he saw it, and the young pilot had certainly showed prowess while flying the unwieldy AVG two-seater. To von Richthofen's delight, he was invited to join Boelcke's embryo fighter squadron on the Somme front.

It was not long before Boelcke learned that his choice had been fully justified. On 17 September 1916 he selected four pilots, including von Richthofen, to accompany him on an offensive patrol. It was *Jagdstaffel* 2's first war flight as a team, using the then new Albatros Scouts. Over the front, the Germans encountered a British formation consisting of eight bomb-carrying BE 2cs escorted by six FE 2b two-seater scouts. After stalking the British machines for some distance, Boelcke led his pilots into the attack. Von Richthofen, after making one ill-judged firing pass at an FE during which he almost came to grief, remembered what Boelcke had taught him and made another approach, creeping up beneath his opponent in the observer's blind spot. When the range was close enough he opened fire, raking the underside of the FE's fuselage nacelle. His bullets shattered the FE's engine and mortally wounded both observer and pilot. The latter, regaining a measure of control, made a successful forced landing. Von Richthofen, unable to restrain himself, landed alongside and reached the British aircraft just as German soldiers were lifting out the blood-stained bodies of the two airmen. The observer opened his eyes as von Richthofen bent over him, smiled, and died. The pilot was rushed to a nearby dressing station, but was dead on arrival. Somewhat sobered, von Richthofen climbed back into his Albatros and flew back to *Jasta* 2's base at Lagnicourt.

Boelcke's untimely death in October 1916 (see chapter two) made the young pilots he had nurtured fiercely determined to carry on his tradition, and with the training he had given them some of their individual scores began to mount quickly – so quickly, in fact, that bets were laid on the date when Boelcke's final tally of forty would be surpassed. By the middle of November 1916 von Richthofen's score stood at thirteen – and there it nearly stopped, for a few days later, on the 23rd, Richthofen fought what he later described as the toughest air battle of his whole career.

His opponent was the leading RFC ace of the day, Major Lanoe George Hawker, officer commanding No 24 Squadron, who was flying an Airco DH 2 single-seat scout. An experienced pilot who had learned to fly before the war, Hawker had first achieved fame by bombing the German Zeppelin sheds at Cologne from a height of only 200 feet. Later, he had become the first pilot to destroy three enemy aircraft in a single day, a feat that earned him the Victoria Cross. Von Richthofen, who described the ensuing battle with supreme arrogance in his diary, encountered Hawker when the latter, flying with two other machines, broke away and dived on the German, who was flying alone.

> 'The Englishman tried to catch me up in the rear while I tried to get round behind him. So we circled round and round like madmen after one another at an altitude of about 10,000 feet. First we circled twenty times to the left, and then thirty times to the right. Each tried to get behind and above the other.
>
> When we had got down to about 6,000 feet without having achieved anything particular, my opponent ought to have discovered that it was time for him to take his leave. The wind was favourable for me, for it drove us more and more towards the German positions. At last we were above Bapaume, about half a mile behind the German front. The gallant fellow was full of pluck, and when we had got down to about 3,000 feet he merrily waved at me as if to say, "Well, how do you do?"
>
> 'The circles which we made around one another

Above: The Halberstadt CL II was the first German two-seater designed specifically for close support and ground attack.

were so narrow that their diameter was probably no more than 250 or 300 feet. I had time to take a good look at my opponent. I looked down into his cockpit and could see every movement of his head. If he had not had his helmet on I would have seen what kind of face he was making.

'My Englishman was a good sportsman, but by and by the thing became a little too hot for him. He had to decide whether he would land on German ground or whether he would fly back to the English lines. Of course he tried the latter, after having endeavoured in vain to escape me by loopings and such tricks. At that time his first bullets were flying around me, for so far neither of us had been able to do any shooting. When he had come down to about 300 feet he tried to escape by flying a zig-zag course, which makes it difficult for an observer on the ground to shoot. That was my most favourable moment. I followed him at an altitude of from 250 to 150 feet, firing all the time. The Englishman could not help falling. But the jamming of my gun had robbed me of success.

'My opponent fell, shot through the head 150 feet behind our lines. His machine-gun was dug out of the ground and it ornaments the entrance of my dwelling . . .'

At the end of the year Richthofen, who had now destroyed sixteen aircraft, was given command of his own squadron, *Jagdstaffel* 11. The fact did not especially please him, as he recorded: 'I must say I was annoyed. I had learnt to work so well with my comrades of Boelcke's squadron, and now I had to begin all over again working hand in hand with different people. It was a beastly nuisance.' Nevertheless, his annoyance was tempered a few days later by the news that he had been awarded the *Pour le Mérite*.

Now that he was in command of his own unit, and consequently in a position to authorize all flights himself, von Richthofen flew at every available opportunity. His score increased by leaps and bounds, as did his self-confidence; the latter was shaken slightly in March 1917, when his fuel tank was holed at 9,000 feet and he glided down to make a forced landing, expecting to burst into flames all the while, but he was soon back in action again and by the end of the month his score stood at thirty-nine.

In August 1917, Richthofen's *Jagdgeschwader* – as it had now become, with an establishment of four *Jagdstaffeln* – re-equipped with Fokker Triplanes, enabling it to hold its own against the growing numbers of Sopwith Camels now serving with the RFC squadrons in France. By the end of the year the *Geschwader*'s strength had increased to five *Staffeln* – about sixty aircraft – and the morale and efficiency of its pilots remained as high as ever. Von Richthofen's personal score was now sixty-three, and he was the idol of Germany; the cult that grew around him far overshadowed the hero-worship that had surrounded Boelcke and Immelmann.

Von Richthofen's rules for air fighting were simple enough. 'Never shoot holes in a machine,' was his dictum. 'Aim for the man and don't miss him. If you are fighting a two-seater, get the observer first; until you have silenced the gun don't bother about the pilot.' He followed his own advice with ruthless efficiency; there were bullet holes in the bodies of most of his victims.

He brought the same kind of ruthless approach to the training of new pilots. Having satisfied himself that a replacement could handle a Fokker competently, he would literally throw him in at the deep end, ordering him to go off and shoot down an Englishman. Some young pilots inevitably failed to return from these lone sorties, but those who came back had learned more about air fighting in an hour than weeks of practice could have taught them.

Although his prowess in the air remained undiminished, a marked change came over von Richthofen during the early weeks of 1918. Some said he had never been quite the same since suffering a head wound in July the previous year. A lone wolf at the best of times – a fact that made his superlative grasp of teamwork and tactics even more remarkable – he took to spending more and more time on his own, retiring to his room early in the evening to be alone with his thoughts. Friends noted that (like Mick Mannock) he seemed to have become obsessed with the idea of dying by fire, commenting often on the number of his opponents who went down in flames.

At 10.30 on 21 April, von Richthofen set out on what was to be his last mission, flying westwards over the valley of the Somme at the head of fifteen Triplanes. It was not long before they sighted a likely prey: two RE 8 observation aircraft of No 3 Squadron AFC, engaged in counter-battery work. Four Triplanes broke away and dived down to attack them through a barrage of fire put up by British anti-aircraft guns.

A couple of miles away, Roy Brown saw the white puffs of the shell bursts and turned to investigate; a few moments later he picked out the two REs, being severely harassed by the Triplanes, and led his eight Camels at full throttle to their rescue. Overhead, the remaining Triplane pilots waited for an opportune moment to dive down and join the fray as soon as the Camels had committed themselves to engaging their four colleagues.

One of the Camel pilots going into action for the first time was an old school friend of Brown's, Lieutenant Wilfred R. May, better known to his fellow pilots as 'Wop'. Brown had told him not to get mixed up in a general dogfight, if one chanced to develop, but to stay on the fringes and get in a shot if the opportunity presented itself. Now, as he watched the other Camels start their attack, May picked out a Fokker that looked like a sitting target and dived after it. He closed on it and opened fire, missing his target by a hopeless margin in his excitement and inexperience. As he tried to correct his aim his guns jammed; in his enthusiasm he had kept the triggers depressed for too long and the weapons had overheated. He had no alternative but to break off the pursuit and dive away towards the sanctuary of the British lines, again obeying Brown's earlier instructions.

From his vantage point above the mêlée, Richthofen had seen the lone Camel break away. It was just the moment he had been waiting for, the kind of situation that had brought him so many victims. Putting his Triplane into a shallow dive, he positioned himself on May's tail and gradually overhauled the British aircraft. Up above, *Leutnant* Hans Wolff, whose task it was to guard Richthofen's tail at all times, was alarmed on seeing his leader diving towards the British lines and prepared to go after him. At that moment, however, he was attacked by a Camel and had to take evasive action. By the time he had shaken off his opponent he had lost sight of the scarlet Triplane.

The first hint that May had of the doom descending on him was the rattle of Richthofen's machine-guns. Later, he confessed to a feeling of sick horror as he twisted in his seat and saw the scarlet Triplane only yards behind, the black-helmeted head of its pilot clearly visible behind the gunsight. He flung the Camel into a steep turn but failed to shake off his pursuer; Richthofen was too wily a hand to be thrown off by basic manoeuvres of that sort.

High above, Roy Brown, who had been involved in a dogfight with several enemy fighters, suddenly found himself alone. Looking down, he saw May's Camel and the scarlet triplane twisting and weaving along the Somme valley. Without hesitation, he dived down to the aid of his friend. By this time, May was virtually exhausted. Richthofen continued to fire in economical short bursts, his bullets ripping through the fabric of the Camel's wings and sending up flurries of spray from the river below. The speeding aircraft were now down to less than 200 feet as they flew along the course of the Somme. May said later:

> 'Just near Corbie, von Richthofen beat me to it and came over the hill. At that point I was a sitting duck; I was too low down between the banks to make a turn away from him. I felt that he had me cold, and I was in such a state of mind at this time that I had to restrain myself from pushing the stick forward and diving into the river, as I knew that I had had it.'

Brown arrived just in time, pulling out of his dive above and slightly to the right of the Fokker. Correcting with rudder, he got the Triplane squarely in his sights and opened fire with his twin Vickers. Bullets stitched a trail of holes along the Triplane's fuselage. Richthofen looked around, and Brown clearly saw what he took to be an expression of startled fear on the face behind the goggles. A moment later, the German pilot slumped sideways in the cockpit. The Fokker swerved violently, then righted itself and nosed over into a glide. It hit the ground and bounced, shedding a wheel, then slid to a halt the right way up two miles inside the British lines, close to some Australian trenches.

Not only Brown had fired at von Richthofen. Near Corbie, two Australians of the 24th Machine Gun Company – Sergeant C.B. Popkin and Gunner R.F. Weston – had loosed off a long burst at the Triplane as it flew low past them in pursuit of May. A few seconds later, two anti-aircraft Lewis guns of the 53rd Battery, 14th Australian Field Artillery Brigade, manned by Gunners W.J. Evans and R. Buie, had also fired on it. Later, all these men were to claim the credit for shooting down von Richthofen.

The Triplane's heavy landing was witnessed by Sergeant-Major J.H. Sheridan of the 3rd Battery, Royal Artillery, who had been watching the chase. Sheridan waited for the German pilot to climb out, but when there was no movement the soldier ran forward and peered into the cockpit. The pilot was slumped forward, his head resting against the breech of one of the Spandau machine-guns. One hand still gripped the stick. Blood oozed from his mouth and from a hole in his chest where a bullet had made its exit, having traversed his body after entering the right side. There was no doubt that he was dead.

The next day, a British aircraft flew over the German airfield at Cappy and dropped a message. It read: 'To the German Flying Corps. *Rittmeister* Baron von Richthofen was killed in aerial combat on 21 April 1918. He was buried with full military honours. From the British Royal Air Force.'

Manfred von Richthofen's body was later removed to a German war cemetery, and in 1925 it was finally laid to rest in Berlin. Roy Brown flew several more missions before being sent to England, where he was admitted to hospital suffering from severe stomach trouble and nervous strain. After the war he went back to Canada and became a businessman. He died in 1944 at the age of fifty, having never fully recovered his health. Lieutenant W.R. May went on to score thirteen victories and win a Distinguished Flying Cross; he too went back to Canada, where he took up a career in civil aviation. He died in 1952.

Although Roy Brown was officially credited with the killing of von Richthofen, no one knows to this day whose bullet sent him down. Except to adherents of the 'Red Baron cult' which has grown over the years along with an upsurge of interest in First World War aviation, the fact of who killed him is unimportant. What was important was the profound effect that the death of the seemingly invincible von Richthofen had

Below: RAF personnel examining the Spandau guns salvaged from the wreck of von Richthofen's Fokker Triplane.

on millions of Germans, soldiers and civilians alike. According to General Ludendorff, the psychological impact of his death was equivalent to the loss of thirty divisions. The Richthofen *Geschwader* continued to fight hard under new commanders, but the loss of von Richthofen's personal leadership was noticeable. For the German Flying Corps, it was as though that day in April 1918 marked the start of the slide into final defeat.

It almost marked the end of Ludendorff's aspirations on the Somme, too, although in April the Germans had made a desperate final effort to gain the upper hand by switching the focus of their attacks against the British Second Army, covering the Ypres-Amentières sector in the north, on the Lys, with the object of breaking through to the vital supply ports of Calais and Boulogne. The Second Army now included the remnants of the Fifth; the British First Army lay to the south, on the right flank, with French forces separating the two along a few miles of the front

The pattern of the German attack, and the air operations that accompanied it, were similar to those that had unfolded on the Somme, although in many ways the British situation on the Lys was more perilous. The few miles between the front and the Channel coast allowed no room for manoeuvre and the area was crammed with supply dumps and airfields, whose loss would have been immediately fatal. The first German objective was the railway station before Hazebrouck, and at one time the enemy spear-heads were within four miles of it. Only a stout resistance in the north, and a very gallant and costly stand by the 55th West Lancashire Division at Givenchy, on the southern flank, prevented the total disintegration of the Allied line.

Conditions on the Lys were different from those on the Somme. The countryside around the Lys was a maze of lanes, streams, canals and dykes, and flying conditions were more arduous. The March weather had given way to mist that hung heavily over the damp Flanders plain, and there were frequent squalls of snow and sleet. Nevertheless, the British air effort, although not as sustained as it had been during March, had its effect on the enemy, as extracts from the German war diaries for the mid-April period once again reveal.

> 'The battalions all suffered severely during their approach march from the British low flying aircraft which attacked them savagely with machine-gun fire and bombs . . . The attack did not take place . . . but the tired, worn-out troops, closely packed together, suffered heavily from the bombs and machine-guns of enemy aeroplanes.'

And, in the words of General von Arnim, commanding the German First Army:

> 'Everywhere I heard complaints about the heavy losses caused by bombing attacks, especially in horses, which had no protection.'

On 21 April, four weeks after they had begun under such terrible pressure, the great Allied retreats of spring 1918 ended, and by the end of the month the Allied lines were consolidating into strong trench systems. On the Somme, the last German attack was made on 24 April when they captured Villers Bretonneux and Hangard, but the Australians retook these objectives the following night. The Germans had played their last card in a final bid to take Amiens, and they had lost.

Chapter Eight

New types, new challenges

On 6 May 1918, sixteen SPADs of SPA.57, led by Lt Jean Chaput, were patrolling in support of the French Eighth Army on the Oise when the Frenchmen encountered a formation of German aircraft of a type they had not seen before. Chaput, who had gained his sixteenth combat victory on 21 April, the day von Richthofen was killed, led his pilots into the attack. They claimed five enemy aircraft destroyed, but the encounter left them completely exhausted and they knew that the German type was likely to prove a formidable opponent. One by one the SPAD pilots straggled back to base, discovering to their dismay that Jean Chaput was missing. Troops in the French front line reported that they had seen a SPAD spiralling down from the combat to make a heavy landing in no-man's land; it was Chaput's machine and the pilot was dead, with three bullets in his body.

The enemy biplane, it turned out, was the Fokker D VII, the first of a series of new German fighter types which – had they been available in numbers several weeks earlier – might have wrested air superiority from the Allies during the Ludendorff offensives. The Fokker D VII was

Above and Below: The Fokker D VII, held by many to be the finest fighter aircraft of WWI.

the first of them, and had its origins late in 1917, at a time when the German Flying Corps was beginning to lose the ascendency and technical superiority it had enjoyed for nearly three years. The German High Command considered the situation to be so serious that it ordered German aircraft manufacturers to give top priority to the development of new fighter types; the prototypes of the various designs would take part in a competitive fly-off at Johannisthal, and the winning firm would receive large production contracts for its aircraft.

Anthony Fokker's contender, the D VII fighter biplane, was completed in November 1917 with rather more haste than its designer would have wished, as he explained later.

> 'The competition date arrived several days sooner than I found desirable. I was working day and night on the plane, but in order to be represented at all I had hurriedly to finish off a model considerably short of what I had in mind. It was a biplane and, in deference to conservatism, the wings were connected near the tips by single 'N' struts. The fuselage section I left square to facilitate manufacture. I retained the tiny aerofoil surface (which had characterized the D VI and other Fokker scouts) which streamlined the landing gear axle, and the whole plane was designed around the 160 hp Mercedes six-cylinder motor, for it was part of the competition rules that every entrant should use this engine – the only one available in quantity. With only just enough time to make a sketchy test hop at Schwerin to determine whether my plane would fly at all, we loaded it on to a truck and raced to Johannisthal.'

Fokker's brief maiden flight in the D VII had shown that it had excellent all-round potential, but that it was far too responsive on the controls, particularly in tight turns, resulting in a tendency to flick into a spin unless its pilot handled it with great sensitivity. The rules of the competition permitted manufacturers to demonstrate their entries either personally or with an officially-appointed test pilot, and Fokker had taken advantage of this on the first few days to make a thorough assessment of the aircraft's faults. Later on in the fly-off, the manufacturers were to be barred from Johannisthal while their designs were put through their paces by operational pilots, who would report on their respective fighting qualities. As it turned out, Fokker was the only manufacturer who had elected to fly his own aircraft during the initial phase.

> 'I flew each day, learning as much about the ship as possible, and showing by direct comparison that it would out-perform any other plane in the sky. Keeping it well in hand, watching its tricks, I played with the other pilots, diving on them, circling them, swooping in under their tails, looping around them, driving their planes down to earth and in general enjoying myself to the utmost while displaying my ship to best advantage. The manoeuvrability of my plane in short, sharp turns at low altitudes was particularly impressive. At the same time I began to realize that if one of the operational pilots took the ship up in its present form and endeavoured to emulate my performance, he would probably kill himself. Finally, I concluded that the fuselage lacked sufficient rear side area, had too much front side area, and that the fin and rudder were too small. Something had to be done for, on Monday, the planes were to be turned over to the operational pilots.
>
> 'That Saturday I telephoned Schwerin for two of my best welders to come at once. As soon as night fell we locked ourselves in the dim hangar to reconstruct the ship. In its cavernous depths we laboured like gnomes under the violet glare of acetylene torches, cutting through the fuselage to weld in another bay of two feet, and enlarging the fin in equal ratio. It was a long, exhausting job all through the night and lasting until Sunday noon. In the end the fabric was patched so smoothly that nothing appeared to have been done to the ship.

Weary though I was, I had yet to take my ship up once more to determine whether the alterations had remedied its faults. In the main they had. The fighter was no longer dangerous to a pilot, although it still swung around corners at a fast clip. Properly employed, this characteristic was an asset. The spinning tendency had disappeared . . . in the hands of an experienced pilot, aware of its weakness, the sensitivity of control became its strength.

'With a lighter heart I landed, and next day my plane was turned over to the Contest Committee. Before leaving the field for good, however, I sauntered over to a group of pilots who were waiting to test the various planes. I pulled *Oberleutnant* Bruno Lörzer, who commanded a front-line *Jagdstaffel*, to one side. 'You'll notice a special feature of my ship, *Herr Leutnant*,' I said, 'its quickness in turns. Let the others in on it so that they can show it off to best advantage.' Then I left, having put them on their guard without their realizing it, ostensibly to seek some much-needed sleep.

'With that little tip, they demonstrated the plane as well as or better than I could have done myself. At altitude the plane's performance was particularly good because of the thick wing, and this factor was highly important.'

The wily Fokker had no intention of missing the fly-off. Just before it was due to begin, he took off from the far side of the aerodrome in an old experimental aircraft which he had planted there earlier and climbed to 15,000 feet to watch the proceedings.

'I was delighted with the manner in which the Fokker was showing up the others. None of my chief competitors, the Rumpler, the LFG, the Albatros or the Pfalz was in the running. The pilots, following Lörzer's tip-off, flew my ship in much the same way as I had done from the first day, playing with the other planes and out-manoeuvring

Below and following two photographs: The Pfalz D XII was a contender with the Fokker D VII for large production orders, but was produced only in limited numbers.

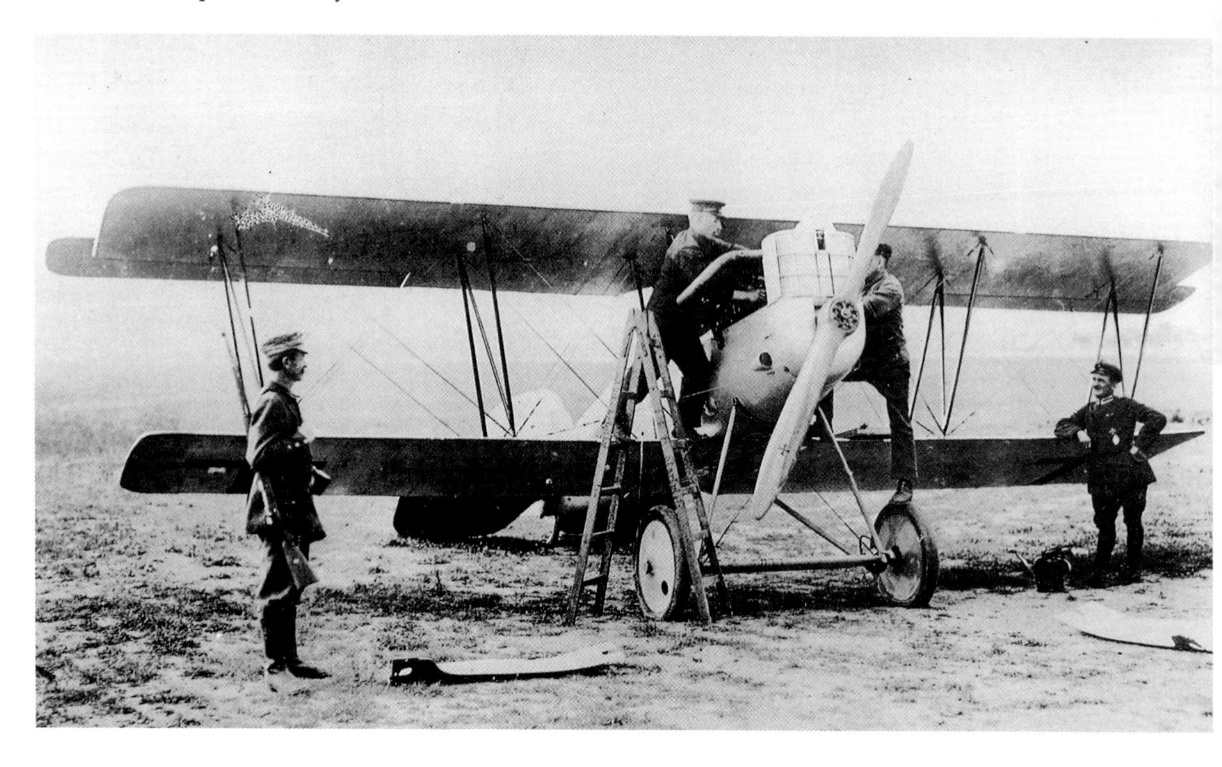

them all the way down from 15,000 to 1,000 feet, displaying in every way the unmistakeable superiority of the Fokker. The Rumpler was much faster and had a nice climb but suffered a rather high wing loading. It was my most dangerous competitor. The arrangement of the radiators on the fuselage sides, however, disturbed the airflow around the control surfaces so that it handled badly at awkward moments. Otherwise it was a clean ship and gave a good account of itself.'

By the fourth day of the fly-off there was no longer any doubt that the Fokker was by far the best all-round design, superior to the other competitors on every count except, perhaps, rate of climb. The Rumpler D I tended to lose height in turns at high altitude while the Fokker stayed firmly under control; the Albatros D VI was almost a duplicate of the earlier D V and showed no improvement, the Pfalz D XII showed dangerous structural weaknesses, the Roland-designed LFG D VI had very poor visibility from the cockpit, and the AEG contender was a hopeless failure all round.

Although the fly-off ended with Fokker confident that his D VII had beaten the other designs hands down, he was astonished when *Hauptmann* Falkenhayn, adjutant to the German Flying Corps C-in-C General von Höppner, asked him to quote a price for the production of 400 aircraft. Up to that time, the largest order

Fokker had received for any of his fighter designs had been for sixty Dr I triplanes. Recovering himself quickly and doing some fast mental arithmetic, he told the adjutant that the total cost would be ten million marks. Falkenhayn agreed without hestitation, and told Fokker that the Albatros factory was to build the new aircraft on a royalty basis.

Fokker admitted later that he was stunned.

> 'Although all efforts had been directed towards staging a comeback, the thoroughness of it rather swept me off my feet. After nearly a year as the front-line favourite, the Albatros was scrapped and the army was forcing the Albatros *Werke* to build my plane on a five percent royalty basis. Soon the so-called Hindenburg Programme was to come into effect, calling for an enormous expansion of the air arm, and the AEG factory was also to be ordered to build my D VII.'

Despite all the priority given to the production of the D VII, it took time to set up the necessary machinery and it was not until the last days of April 1918 that the first examples were delivered to *Jagdgeschwader* 1, which was now commanded by *Hauptmann* Wilhelm Reinhard. The new aircraft cost Reinhard his life, for he was accidentally killed while flying one a few days later. So JG.1 received its third and last commanding officer, a leader of proven worth who now had twenty victories to his credit and who wore the *Pour le Mérite*: Hermann Göring.

For the other contenders in the fighter competition, there was a small consolation; pre-production orders were awarded to the respective companies for fifty examples each of the Rumpler D I and the Roland D VI, while Pfalz received an order for the construction of 200 D XIIs.

Another firm that received a small order was the Siemens-Schuckert *Werke* (SSW), who were contracted to build sixty examples of their D III scout. Believed by some German pilots to be the best fighter at the front in the summer of 1918, the SSW D III was a stubby, compact little biplane of wooden construction powered by a 160 hp Siemens-Halske rotary engine. During flight trials in October 1917, the prototype D III had reached a level speed of 112 mph and climbed to 19,600 feet in less than twenty minutes, a performance which justified its being ordered into immediate production. At the same time, the *IDFLIEG – Inspektion der Fliegertruppen* – placed small orders for two further developments, the D IV and D V.

The first batch of thirty SSW D III scouts was delivered for operational trials in January 1918, and in February the *IDFLIEG* ordered thirty more aircraft. Beginning in late April, forty-one examples were allocated to operational units on the Western Front; most of these went to JG 2, which equipped its *Jasta* 15 with the type. The pilots were delighted with the new aircraft, and a typical verdict on the SSW D III was that it was highly sensitive on the controls, possessed excellent flying qualities and climbed like a rocket.

One German ace who was a firm advocate of the SSW D III was *Hauptmann* Rudolf Berthold, a talented pilot who had begun his combat career with *Fliegerabteilung* 23 in 1916, scoring his first victories while flying a Fokker Monoplane. He survived a series of close shaves – including a tricky forced landing after a fight with three BE 2cs and a crash while testing a Pfalz Scout – and in October 1916, while commanding *Jasta* 14, he gained his tenth victory and was awarded the *Pour le Mérite*. In August 1917 he assumed command of *Jasta* 18, and in one month he destroyed fourteen RFC aircraft before being shot down himself and severely wounded in the right arm.

Returning to action in the spring of 1918, he took command of JG 2, which comprised *Jasta*s 12, 13, 15 and 19. When JG 2 received the Fokker D VII, he had his aircraft specially modified so that he could fly and fight with his one good hand and the limited use of the other. He was in constant pain from his injury and his determination was greatly admired by his fellow pilots, who nicknamed him the 'Iron Knight'. His SSW D III, which he tested in action during the first weeks of May 1918, was distinctively painted with a red and blue engine cowling and a flaming sword insignia.

On 23 May 1918, Berthold submitted a report on the aircraft's engine performance to the *IDFLIEG*.

> 'Basically the new Siemens-Halske S.III engine is sound and the pilots have faith in it. One particular advantage is that engine power remains constant even at high altitude. After rectifying the defects reported to the Commanding General of the Air Service by *Jagdgeschwader* 2 on 17 April 1918, and particularly after reducing the control forces and the excessive left-hand torque suffered by the aircraft, the SSW D.III can be considered a perfectly acceptable front-line machine, but the aircraft cannot be used at the present time as, after seven to ten hours' running of the Sh.III engines the pistons seize, the crowns being torn off and the pieces dropping into the crankcase.'

As a result of Berthold's report, the thirty-five SSW D.IIIs then serving with the *Jasta*s were withdrawn from front-line service at the end of May and returned to the Siemens-Schuckert factory for airframe and engine modifications. It was to be two months before they were returned to operational service, and then they were used mainly for home defence duties. *Jasta* 15 reverted to the Fokker D VII, and it was while flying one of these, on 10 August 1918, that Rudolf Berthold scored his last two victories, bringing his total to forty-four. Soon afterwards, in a fight with Sopwith Camels, he was shot down and sustained more injuries; he survived them only to be murdered by German communists in Harburg on 15 December 1919.

Another Fokker design of 1918 that at first appeared to show much promise was the E V (the 'E' denoting *Eindecker*, or monoplane). A very simple design, it had a one-piece cantilever parasol wing and twin Spandau machine-guns mounted immediately in front of the cockpit. Production E Vs were delivered to the German Flying Corps from July 1918, but in August *Jasta* 6, one of the first units to receive the type, experienced three serious crashes due to wing structural failure. Imperfect timber and faulty manufacturing methods were found to have been the cause, but sixty aircraft were immobilized in the factory while investigations were carried out and it was not until September that production was started again, the type now bearing the designation Fokker D VIII. It was more manoeuvrable than the D VII biplane and had a better operational ceiling, although it was slightly slower. Only about ninety had been delivered by the end of the war and, although its pilots reported that it handled well, it had little chance to prove itself in action.

For the German Flying Corps, the introduction of new types in the early summer of 1918 came too late. The will to fight was still there, but the economic resources to sustain it were not. But any illusion the Allies might have harboured about the war coming to a rapid end was soon to be dispelled, for the summer months of 1918 were to witness some of the most bitter and bloody fighting in the history of air warfare. With the failure of the Ludendorff offensives, the Germans could no longer hope for an overwhelming victory. Their fight now was to preserve the integrity of the German Empire, to beat the Allied armies to a standstill, and to secure an honourable peace.

CHAPTER NINE

The Allied recovery, May–June 1918

As the front lines stabilized again in the wake of the great German offensive, massive artillery exchanges became the order of the day, and counter-battery work by observation aircraft on both sides assumed new importance. As a consequence, large air battles developed between the scouts charged with protecting the reconnaissance aircraft, and there was a sharp rise in the personal scores of the leading fighter pilots. By the third week in April, for example, René Fonck's score had risen to thirty-six aircraft destroyed, and he seemed unstoppable. The main reason behind his growing success was that he was meticulous in his approach to air fighting, constantly devising new methods of exercising his heart, muscles and reflexes to cope with the stresses of combat as well as ensuring that his machine and its armament were technically perfect. To reduce the risk of his guns jamming – which had been responsible for the death of many a pilot at a crucial moment in a dogfight – he invented a simple device for checking the calibre of every bullet in his ammunition belts. If there was the slightest sign of imperfection, the bullet was eliminated.

Fonck brought his own brand of science to air combat, spending hours of his leisure time working out such things as relative speeds and deflection angles. He inspected as many shot-down enemy aircraft as possible, not because of any macabre fascination, but because he wanted to work out the blind spots of individual aircraft types. In the air, Fonck's economy in the use of ammunition was almost legendary; he seldom used more than a dozen bullets to despatch an adversary. Correct positioning and superb marksmanship were Fonck's twin secrets; he could hit a five-franc piece with a rifle bullet when most other people could not even see the coin.

Above: An LVG C-type over the front.

He attributed much of his success to the 500 hours he had spent flying reconnaissance machines early in the war. 'You have to be careful when you are attacking a two-seater,' he said, 'and remember that it is armed at both front and rear. Having flown this type of machine for so long I knew exactly what it could do, and how it could always be shot down by a more manoeuvrable single-seater flown by a pilot who knew what he was doing.'

Fonck was one of the first real examples of a new breed of fighter pilot; a cold, calculating scientist for whom amateurism had no place in combat. He worked out every move in the minutest detail, leaving nothing to chance. He knew that lack of attention to detail killed far too many pilots; he had seen many of his friends die because they had not taken sufficient care of their machine guns, or their engine, or because they had drunk too much brandy the night before a patrol. Methodically, he set about reducing the part played by the traditional 'pilot's luck' in his personal survival to the barest minimum.

Nevertheless, he was by no means dispassionate. He gave his novice pilots every encouragement, even crediting his own 'kills' to them. He was never 'kill-conscious', like many of his fellow pilots; what mattered to Fonck was the ability to survive. Once that was assured to the best of his ability, the chances of shooting down Germans would automatically increase.

The proof of his doctrine lay in his ability to shoot down Germans with what appeared to be astonishing ease. On 9 May 1918, for example, he equalled the exploits of the RAF 's John Trollope and Henry Woollett by shooting down six aircraft in one day, the first three in the space of one minute. These were all two-seaters, which he caught flying in formation over Grivèsnes. The first one went down before his guns at 4.05 pm, the next one ten seconds later, and the third after a running battle lasting forty seconds. He landed to refuel and have something to eat; then, on a second patrol, he sighted a formation of Pfalz Scouts and engaged them at 6.40, shooting down the first one almost immediately. He destroyed a second at 6.45, and another ten seconds later. In the destruction of all six aircraft, he had expended just fifty-two rounds of ammunition.

May was also an exceptional month for that other leading exponent of clinical air fighting, Mick Mannock, whose No 74 Squadron was constantly in the forefront of the fighting. His exploits are detailed in the official summary for May 1918.

'May 6th. Captain E. Mannock . . . engaged one EA Triplane and forced it into a spin. He followed the EA down, firing short bursts and the EA finally turned over on its back and crashed.

'May 12th. Captain E. Mannock, 74 Squadron,

Above: An AEG C IV after a landing accident. The C IV, the major variant of AEG's C-types, was produced for armoured ground strafing duties from early 1918.

with his patrol, encountered a formation of eight EA scouts; he attacked the rear machine at close range and at right angles, and the EA side-slipped underneath him and collided with another enemy scout, both enemy machines falling to pieces in the air. Capt Mannock then engaged another EA scout from behind and fired a long burst into it from both guns; the EA went down vertically and was seen to dive into the ground.

'May 16th. Capt E. Mannock, 74 Sqn, fired about 40 rounds at one EA scout which went into a vertical dive and broke to pieces in the air.

'May 17th. Capt E. Mannock . . . attacked the rear machine of a formation of EA scouts and fired a long burst from both guns into it, and the EA spun down out of control. Capt Mannock was then attacked by another EA and forced to spin away, but 210 Squadron confirm the first EA attacked by Capt Mannock as having crashed in flames. Later in the day Capt Mannock observed an EA two-seater crossing the line near Ypres. He climbed north and then east and approached the EA at which he fired approximately 200 rounds at close range during a fight which lasted about one minute, the EA going down alternately diving and spinning. At about 4,000 feet the EA burst into flames and was seen to crash and to burn itself out on the ground.

'May 18th. Capt E. Mannock engaged an enemy two-seater at right angles, firing a burst of 40 rounds into it. The EA went down in a vertical dive and crashed near Steenwerck, and burst into flames on hitting the ground.

'May 21st. A patrol of 74 Squadron encountered six Pfalz Scouts, upon whom they dived, shooting down five of them – of which Major K.L. Caldwell destroyed one, Captain E. Mannock three, and

Above: Captured Albatros D III. This photograph was taken in the Middle East.

Above: Albatros D III of No 2 (Naval) *Jagdstaffel* pictured over Flanders.

Captain W.E. Young one. Captain Mannock also destroyed another EA earlier in the day.'

Mannock's prowess in combat was a fine example to the younger pilots of No 74 Squadron, and they had great faith and pride in him as a leader. One of them was Lt Ira 'Taffy' Jones, who was to end the war with a score of 40 enemy aircraft destroyed. Jones gained his first victory on 8 May and ran up a steady score during the remainder of the month. On the 9th he drove an Albatros down out of control (which would have been classed as a 'probable' in the Second World War) and on the 17th, with his patrol, attacked ten Pfalz Scouts. During the ensuing battle he saw a two-seater slightly in front of and just below him, and opened fire with both guns. He saw hits on the engine and both cockpits and the enemy went down vertically, trailing smoke and eventually bursting into flames, to crash near Estaires.

On the following day, Jones engaged a two-seater which was flying through anti-aircraft fire, and put 250 rounds into it from beneath its tail. There was an explosion and the enemy aircraft caught fire and crashed. More anti-aircraft bursts led him to another two-seater over Hazebrouck; he also attacked this aircraft from below, but ran into heavy defensive fire from its observer, who was shooting through a hole in the fuselage floor. Jones described what happened next:

'Very suddenly (the pilot) tilted his machine very steeply, and it seemed as if a black object had been deliberately thrown at me. I thought at first it was the observer's gun, so I slithered quickly to the other side and as I did so, looked for the object. To my amazement, I saw the body of the observer, falling with arms outstretched and legs wide apart, and going down in a series of tumbling circles. It was a horrifying sight. He fell in the trenches near Meteren.'

On 25 May, Jones noted in his diary:

'The CO saved Giles' skin today. Giles very carelessly allowed a black Albatros to pounce on him while he was concentrating on the destruction of a silver-grey two-seater. Giles has had his leg pulled unmercifully; we declare he was decoyed. Pilots hate admitting that they have been taken in as a sucker!'

The Giles mentioned by Jones was Lt W.B. Giles, who on 12 May, in the words of the official summary, had:

'Dived on an EA scout and fired bursts from both guns into it. The EA turned over on its back but recovered close to the ground and flew east very low as if to land. Observing this, Lt Giles dived on the EA from 5,000 feet and fired a further burst into it. The EA dived and made off east. (This EA has been confirmed as having crashed in the vicinity of Wulverghem by another pilot of 74 Sqn.)'

Jones's diary continues.

'Clements tells me that Mick saved his life tonight, too. Mick and Clements[1] were up for a bit of fun after tea. They each got what they wanted . . . Clements spotted a large formation of Huns obviously making a beeline for them. Clements put on full throttle . . . to catch up to Mick, who as usual was wasting no time in getting at his enemy. Mick had seen the Hun formation all the time . . . he turned west quickly and dived, the Huns following and firing. Mick saved Clements by losing height directly beneath them and so drawing them on to him, while Clements got clear. Clements says it was a rotten sight to see one S.E. being attacked by such a bunch, and that had it been anyone except Mick, he would have been anxious about his safety. (We all believe that no Hun will ever shoot down Mick.) One Pfalz followed him very closely, and suddenly Mick went down out of control; on his back – spinning – and doing everything imaginable from 8,000 to 4,000 feet. At 5,000 feet the Hun, completely fooled, flattened out to watch the crash. Mick then decided he had had enough, and flattened out too and made for our lines – diving hard.'

[1] Lt H.G. Clements

Another pilot whose score increased rapidly during the heavy air fighting of May 1918 was Captain A.W. Beauchamp-Proctor of No 84 Squadron (SE 5as, Bertangles), a South African who was to end the war with fifty-four victories, making him the fifth-ranking British ace. On 10 May Beauchamp-Proctor stalked a two-seater which he had sighted climbing for altitude as it approached the British lines and fired fifty rounds into it, killing the observer. He then closed in and opened fire again, at which the two-seater went into a vertical dive. The RAF pilot watched it fall through 4,000 feet until it was lost to sight in the haze, but another 84 Squadron pilot confirmed that it had crashed.

On 15 May Beauchamp-Proctor took off on a pre-dawn sortie in an attempt to intercept enemy bombers that had been attacking Amiens. He failed to find them, so flew east in the hope of catching them over their airfield as they returned from their bombing mission. He had no difficulty in finding the enemy aerodrome, where landing flares had been lit. Throttling back, he glided down to 3,000 feet, then circled a few miles to the west to await events. A few minutes later a twin-engined aircraft, probably a Gotha, flew just over him and he turned to attack it, but its gunner was on the alert and opened fire. Proctor fired in turn, and the German gunner fell silent. Then Proctor's own guns jammed, and by the time he had cleared the stoppage the bomber was almost over its airfield.

Beauchamp-Proctor closed in again and renewed his fire, seeing the enemy aircraft discharge a red flare, which was answered from the ground. The next instant the airfield's defences opened up and the RAF pilot found himself flying through a storm of heavy machine-gun fire and tracer shells. At 2,000 feet he was forced to break off the combat, having driven the enemy aircraft some distance away from the aerodrome. When he last saw the bomber it was in a dive, and although it was still under control it had almost certainly suffered heavy damage.

In fact, Beauchamp-Proctor was to share fifth place at the end of hostilities with another pilot: a Canadian, Captain D.M. MacLaren of No 46 Squadron, which in mid-May 1918 flew Sopwith Camels from Liettres. MacLaren's first success in May came on the 3rd, when he fired 75 rounds into a two-seater from a range of fifty yards and sent it down in flames. Almost immediately afterwards he shared in the destruction of a second two-seater with another 46 Squadron pilot, 2nd Lt V.M. Yeates. On 6 May MacLaren and Yeates, together with three other 46 Squadron pilots, harried another two-seater to destruction, and in the same week MacLaren drove two more enemy machines down out of control, but was unable to claim them as confirmed victories. A few days later he shared another with Lt C.R. Chapman, and on 20 May he shot two enemy observation balloons down in flames.

Major Roderic Dallas of No 40 Squadron (SE 5as) lost no time in opening his May air fighting account, shooting down a Pfalz Scout on the morning of the 2nd. Later in the day he carried out a daring low-level attack on the enemy airfield at La Brayelle; after strafing the hangars, he turned and raced back over the aerodrome, dropping a pair of army boots in a parcel and a message which read; 'If you won't come up here and fight, herewith one pair of boots for work on the ground. Pilots – for the use of.' Circling in the haze, he waited until a party of Germans had gathered to examine the package and then made another low-level run, firing 100 rounds of ammunition and dropping two 20 lb Cooper bombs. To round off a very satisfactory day's work, he caught an unwary Albatros Scout on its way home and shot it down.

Dallas destroyed two more enemy aircraft in mid-May, and another on the 27th. It was his thirty-ninth and last victory, although according to some sources his true total was fifty-one. His personal SE 5 was well known to the enemy; instead of the drab khaki upper surfaces and cream underside that was the standard RAF colour scheme, he had had it painted in a distinctive green and brown camouflage pattern similar to that which the RAF was to adopt many years later.

On 1 June 1918, Roderic Dallas failed to return from a lone patrol high over the front line. Later, the wreckage of his aircraft was found near the village of Lieven. According to a German account published later, he had dived on a Fokker Triplane, unaware that it was decoy. Two more had pounced on him, riddling his body with bullets.

Captain R.A. Little of No 203 Squadron also scored his last victory – his forty-seventh – in May. On the 22nd, after shooting down an enemy scout, he was on his way home after being forced to leave his patrol because of oil pressure trouble when he encountered an Albatros C V two-seater. He attacked it at close range and sent it down at St Leger, seeing it crash in a railway cutting. The next day, the Australian pilot was shot down and killed in the course of an offensive patrol.

Other leading RAF scorers in May were Major James Gilmour of No 56 Squadron (Sopwith Camels, Bertangles) and Lt A.C. Atkey of No 22 Squadron (Bristol Fighters, Serny). On 2 May Gilmour destroyed a couple of two-seaters, and on the 9th he shot down another and damaged a fourth. On the following day he and his patrol attacked a lone Albatros Scout and shared in its destruction, and on 18 May he led his patrol in an engagement with twelve enemy fighters, causing one to break up with his first burst of fire. Soon afterwards he dived on a two-seater and fired a long burst into it; it turned away eastwards and went into a long dive, then crashed to the ground and burst into flames.

Atkey, who had previously flown DH 4s with No 18 Squadron and who had been awarded an MC in April, was posted to No 22 Squadron at the end of the month and teamed up with 2nd Lt C.G. Gass as his observer. They proved to be a formidable team, as an air battle of 7 May showed. That morning, Atkey and Gass were in company with another Bristol Fighter, patrolling in showery weather, when they ran into a formation of seven Albatros and Pfalz Scouts in the vicinity of Henin-Lietard. The two Bristols – the second aircraft was crewed by Lts J.E. Gurdon and A.J.H. Thornton – immediately initiated an attack, but the odds proved to be much heavier than had been anticipated, for the original enemy formation was quickly reinforced by two others which brought the number of enemy aircraft involved to twenty. During a dogfight that lasted half an hour, Atkey and Gass shot down two enemy aircraft in flames and saw three more crash, while Gurdon and Thornton disposed of three more, two of them in flames. The remainder did not stay to fight. Of all battles, this one proved conclusively that the Bristol Fighter, in expert hands, could more than hold its own against a far superior enemy force.

On 9 May Atkey and Gass destroyed another enemy scout, and on a second patrol that day they carried out a single-handed attack on a formation of eight enemy machines. Atkey fired fifty rounds into one at close range; flames burst from the fuselage behind the pilot's seat and it went down to crash. Later in the week they drove three more enemy aircraft down out of control, and on 19 May they shot down a two-seater near Douai. During the next few days they drove four more Germans down out of control, and rounded off the month with a spirited engagement on the 25th. In the words of the official record:

'A patrol of 22 Squadron, led by Captain A.C. Atkey and 2nd Lt C.G. Gass, while escorting DH 4s of 18 Squadron, encountered a large formation of about 40 EA. A fierce fight ensued, in the course of which so many EA were seen spinning and diving away that it was impossible to tell whether they were out of control or not. At the conclusion of the fight four EA were seen crashed on the ground, and in addition, one Albatros Scout, attacked by Lt S.F.H. Thompson and Sgt R.M. Fletcher, was seen to go down in flames.'

Mick Mannock, too, ended May in fine style, as Ira Jones recorded. On 29 May:

'Mick took Clements and me up at 7.00 pm . . . Mick spotted about a dozen Huns coming from the direction of Roubaix; we were then over Lille. As we had not too much time for a fight, having already been up for over an hour, he decided to go straight at them, as we had a slight advantage of height. The Huns, who were Albatros Scouts, were of the stout variety, and they accepted our challenge. Both Mick and the Hun leader opened fire at one another as they approached from about 300 yards' range, but nothing happened. This burst of fire was the signal for a glorious dogfight – as fine and as frightening a dogfight as I've ever been in. Friend and foe fired at and whistled past one another at a tornado pace . . . I have never been so frightened in my life. Of late I have been able to keep very cool during the actual fight, but tonight I became so flustered that occasionally I fired at my own pals in an effort not to miss a chance – thank God, my shooting was erratic. How terrible it would have been if I had, say, shot Mick down. The very thought gives me the creeps . . . Mick sent two slate-blue Albatros down out of control, and Clements crashed his first Hun. He is very bucked about it. It is wonderful how cheered a pilot becomes after he shoots down his first machine – his morale increases by at least a hundred per cent. This is why Mick gives Huns away – to raise the morale of the beginner.'

Mick Mannock and René Fonck, it seems, were two of a kind.

The second week of May witnessed a tragedy that might have been averted, had it not been for a lack of co-operation between Allied commanders. Three British divisions, which had suffered particularly heavy losses in the spring fighting, had been sent south to rest and recuperate on the Aisne, and to reinforce the French line in that sector. They were accompanied by a single RAF observation squadron, No 52, with RE 8s. On 22 May the squadron's crews reported large clouds of dust swirling over the roads in the German rear areas, a sure sign of large-scale troop movements. They reported the same phenomenon the next day, and the day after that. The British commander in the area brought the RAF reports to the notice of the general commanding the French Sixth Army, who ignored them.

Soon after midnight on 27 May, one of the heaviest bombardments of the war thundered down on the British divisions and the two French ones in place beside them. The 21st and 25th British Divisions suffered fearsome casualties and the 50th (Tyne-Tees) Division was virtually wiped out. A fourth British division, the 18th, in reserve, remained intact and was thrown into the battle, together with French reserves. By the time the German advance was halted it had penetrated the Allied line to a depth of twelve miles and had reached the Marne. The disaster prompted a stern reminder from the RAF C-in-C, Major-General Salmond, who ordered that in future every likely approach route was to be reconnoitred twice nightly and again just before dawn, the pilots flying at low level. 'The responsibility that the British Army is not surprised,' he stressed, 'is on the Royal Air Force.'

Never again, in this war, would British troops in the field suffer through lack of adequate air reconnaissance; and never again would an Allied commander fail to act upon the information supplied by the crews of the observation aircraft who daily risked their lives over enemy territory.

For the Allied squadrons, late May and early June 1918 was a period of consolidation. Of the 1,232 first-line aircraft on the British inventory in France at the start of the first Ludendorff Offensive on 21 March, 1,000 were destroyed in the four weeks that followed. The total included 195 missing, 695 wrecked and 141 burnt or abandoned as their aerodromes were threatened by the German advance. On the credit side, the RFC/RAF had claimed 354 enemy aircraft shot down and 188 driven down out of control; with French claims added to this, the air combat losses of both sides were probably about equal.

To make good the RAF's losses, fresh squadrons were sent out from England. One of them was No 85, equipped with SE 5as, which arrived at Petite Synthe on 25 May. Its commanding officer was Major W.A. Bishop VC, whose score at that time stood at sixty enemy aircraft destroyed.

Billy Bishop reopened his scoring on 27 May, when he attacked an enemy two-seater over Houthulst Forest. He pursued it, firing as it turned east, and saw both sets of wings and the tail unit break off. The fragments crashed east of Passchendaele. On the 30th he destroyed two more two-seaters, and shot down an Albatros Scout later in the day. On 3 June, however, Brigadier-General Salmond decided that Bishop was too valuable an asset as a leader to have his life continually at risk, and ordered him to return to England in a fortnight's time.

During that fortnight, in a period of twenty-five days, Bishop destroyed a further twelve enemy aircraft, the first on 4 June. On 17 June, his last day in action but one, he destroyed three in the space of thirty minutes with the

Above: Captain W.A. Bishop, VC.

expenditure of only fifty-five rounds of ammunition. His combat report describes the action:

'10.25 am. Staden and Hooglede. 18,000 feet.

(1) Between Staden and Hooglede, 18,000 feet at 10.25 am, I turned back a two-seater who was approaching our lines, finally closing to seventy-five yards. After twenty rounds he burst into flames.

10.50 am. Sailly-sur-Lys. 4,000 feet.

(2) Over Sailly-sur-Lys, 4,000 feet at 10.50 am, seeing one Albatros I zoomed into the edge of a cloud. Albatros passed cloud and I secured position on tail. After fifteen rounds he fell and crashed just south of village.

10.55 am. Laventie (near). 2,000 feet.

(3) After attacking (2) I saw a two-seater EA quite low. I dived at him from the east but he turned and got east of me. After second burst of twenty rounds he fell in a turning dive, then crashed between Laventie and the main road.'

The next day was even more dramatic. Patrolling near Ypres, Bishop sighted and attacked three Pfalz Scouts, one of which he quickly sent down in flames. As the others turned to attack him, two more Pfalz dropped down from the clouds to join the fray. For a few minutes the five machines circled, the Germans endeavouring to box in the lone SE 5. Then, as two of the Pfalz turned towards him, Bishop acted quickly. He dived between them and the two enemy aircraft, tightening their turns, collided with one another and went down in a cloud of wreckage. The other two at once broke off the combat and turned away; Bishop went after them, opening fire on one from 200 yards. His aim was good and the Pfalz went down, bursting into flames as it fell. The other escaped into a cloud.

On 19 June 1918 Bishop left France for good. In just over a year of air combat he had destroyed seventy-two enemy aircraft. During the Second World War, Billy Bishop – by then an air marshal – was placed in charge of recruiting for the Royal Canadian Air Force. For this work he was awarded the CB to add to an already impressive list of decorations. He died of an illness on 11 September 1956.

Another leading RAF pilot who returned to combat during this period was Major Raymond Collishaw of No 203 Squadron, who celebrated his return in the second week of June by shooting down two enemy aircraft, and claimed another a few days later. However, his return coincided with the onset of poor weather, and he was unable to increase his score before the end of the month.

Number 74 Squadron got away to a good start in June, three of its pilots – Mannock, Jones and Clements – destroying eight enemy aircraft between them in the first week. Mannock's three victories, gained on the first day of the month, were all Pfalz Scouts, which he described as 'dark camouflaged with white tails' – a colour scheme adopted by *Jasta* 35. His combat report reads:

'Observed and engaged formation of EA scouts east of Merville. Attacked from the front and above. The highest scout being behind, S.E. opened fire with both guns at point-blank range. The EA's bottom wings fell off and it crashed. Confirmed also by Lts Giles and Birch.

Engaged another EA and after a short vertical burst at close range, this scout burst into flames. Confirmed by all other members of patrol.

Engaged another EA, which was turning towards me on the same level. Fired several short bursts at this machine whilst circling. The EA went into a spin, and disappeared from the fight.'

There is little doubt that, by this time, Mick Mannock was suffering from what would be called combat fatigue in later wars. He was showing all the classic symptoms: sudden rages, bouts of depression, irrational risk-taking. The recurring depression was reflected in a letter to his sister, written early in June 1918:

'Things are getting a bit intense just lately and I don't quite know how long my nerves will last out. I am rather old now, as airmen go, for fighting. Still, one hopes for the best . . . These times are so horrible that occasionally I feel that life is not worth hanging on to myself . . . I am supposed to be going on leave on the nineteenth of this month (if I live long enough) and I shall call at Birmingham to see you all.'

Mannock did live long enough, and went on leave, and in so doing bade farewell to his beloved 74 Squadron. On his return, he was promoted and given command of No 85 Squadron, a post recently vacated by Billy Bishop.

During the first week of June 1918, the RAF claimed the destruction of fifty-six enemy aircraft over the Western Front, with a further twenty-six 'driven down out of control'. These figures are almost certainly exaggerated, as most air combat claims have been since. The figure that can be relied upon is the RAF's admitted loss of twelve aircraft, a relatively low number that speaks for the lack of air activity on most days. The official summary records that enemy activity was slight or below normal in cloudy conditions except on the 6th, when the weather was fine all day. The previous week's RAF loss was twenty-five, and in the following week it rose to thirty-one as the German fighters once again swarmed over Flanders. During this second week, the RAF claimed sixty-three aircraft destroyed and thirty-one 'driven down'.

Among the many noteworthy incidents of the week was a gallant rescue attempt which, unfortunately, went amiss. On the 13th, Captain J.D. Belgrave, together with Lts H.A. Gordon and R.G. Lewis of No 60 Squadron, attacked a two-seater which they sent down, apparently out of control. As Belgrave followed it down into the mist to make sure of it, Gordon noticed that Lewis was losing height, having apparently suffered damage. A few minutes later Lewis landed in enemy territory between Albaincourt and Chaulnes, smashing his undercarriage in the process. Gordon landed successfully nearby just as some German soldiers appeared and began to fire on the stranded aircraft. Gordon jumped from the cockpit and ran over to his colleague's SE 5, shouting at him to get clear and come across to the serviceable aircraft so that he could take off with both of them on board, but he was too late; Lewis was strolling towards the enemy soldiers, seemingly oblivious to the fact that they were still firing and possibly mistaking them for friendly troops. Gordon ran back to his own aircraft and took off, still under fire. He circled the spot and lined up on the body of German troops, intending to fire at them, but then he noticed that Lewis was standing among them

Below: No parachute: a German pilot jumps clear of his blazing Albatros, the fate of all too many pilots in the First World War.

and he did not shoot. Gordon flew back to his base with one of his rudder control cables shot through and a longeron almost shot away.

It was in the summer of 1918 that a certain disaffection began to spread among the RAF's aircrews because of the unneccessary suffering and loss of life caused by the failure of the authorities to issue parachutes to flying personnel. In the early days, primitive parachutes were bulky and heavy, and to wear them would have imposed an unacceptable weight penalty, as well as restricting the pilot's movements. But by 1918, more powerful aero-engines and improved parachute design had done away with such objections, and the RAF's doctrine that the wearing of parachutes would be detrimental to the aggressive spirit of its pilots was frankly nonsensical; exactly the opposite would have been true. Ira Jones, writing of the air battle of 1 June, summed up the feeling:

> 'For ten minutes the ten S.E.s engaged the seven Pfalz; and when the battle ended one enemy had gone down in flames, one had crashed, and one had gone out of control – all to Mick's guns – while we had lost our flight commander (Captain W.J. Cairns). A determined Pfalz got to within 25 yards of him and gave him the gun. His right wing was suddenly seen to break up, the nose of his S.E. dipped viciously, then downwards he spun at a terrific rate. I watched him for a short while, sickness overcoming me. It is a terrible thing to see a pal going to his death . . . I cannot imagine why we have no parachutes.'

Chapter Ten
Bombing operations, summer 1918

In May 1918, the German Flying Corps did what it ought to have done during the crucial weeks of March and April: it launched a determined bombing campaign with the object of disrupting the Allied lines of communication, which in the British sectors were now heavily congested as a consequence of the earlier retreats. On the night of 19/20 May, fifteen Gothas attacked a vital railway bridge over the Canche estuary at Etaples. They failed to hit the target, but their bombs fell on a nearby military hospital, killing 182 patients and injuring 643. The crew of one of the bombers, which had to make a forced landing after being hit by anti-aircraft fire, expressed incredulity that the British authorities had placed a hospital so close to a vital military objective, maintaining that they had no prior knowledge of the hospital's whereabouts. There is no reason to doubt their claim.

On the last night of the month the German bombers had better success against their assigned target, destroying one span of the bridge. The bombers' real success, however, was against the British ammunition and supply dumps. On 19/20 May, in conjunction with the Etaples raid, Gothas dropped some 500 bombs on No 12 Ordnance Depot at Blarges, which contained 27,000 tons of explosives. In all, 6,000 tons were destroyed. One dump containing

Below: Gotha G IIIs ranged alongside a Zeppelin airship shed

Above: The Gotha G II was the *Gothaer Waggonfabrik*'s first production bomber, but it had a short life. Repeated engine crankshaft failures forced its withdrawal. It served mainly on the Eastern Front.

Below: The Friedrichshafen G IIIs of *Kagohl* 1 carried out many night attacks on Allied installations in the Dunkirk area.

mortar bombs received a direct hit and simply vanished, leaving a crater fifty yards wide and ten deep. On the next night the bombers attacked No 20 Ordnance Depot at Seigneville, wiping out 5,600 tons of ammunition, including 69 million small-arms rounds. Now that the Allied line in the north was stabilizing, these losses were severe, although not critical. Had they occurred a few weeks earlier, with the field commanders crying out for supplies of ammunition and equipment to sustain their battered and retreating armies, they would almost certainly have been disastrous.

The night of 20/21 May also saw the last German aircraft raid on Britain. Twenty-eight Gothas and three Giants set out to attack London, and were met by a vastly more effective night fighter force than had been the case four months earlier, at the time of the previous night raids. Seventy-four Camels and SE 5s went up to intercept the bombers, shooting down three Gothas, while the anti-aircraft defences claimed two more and a sixth crashed in Essex after engine failure. It was the biggest loss suffered by the German bombers in a single night's operations over England, and it was to be more than two decades before they came again.

The cessation of attacks on England by heavier-than-air machines meant that fighters could be released for service in the night-fighting role on the Western Front, and on 12 June 1918 No 151 Squadron formed for this purpose at Hainault Farm, combining one flight each from Nos 44, 78 and 112 Squadrons. The first flight of Camels crossed the Channel on 16 June; by the 26th the whole squadron was installed at Famechon, moving to Fontaine-sur-Maye on 2 July. Its first success was achieved by Captain A.B. Yuille, who sighted and attacked a Gotha in the early hours of 25 July. The Gotha crash-landed behind the British lines with both engines out of action and its observer wounded. In the months that followed, No 151 Squadron was to carry out many night interceptions, as well as mounting night intruder operations against the German bomber airfields, and by the end of the war its pilots had claimed the destruction of twenty-six enemy aircraft. It was to remain a night fighter unit for most of its career, and the last aircraft it used in this role in the late 1950s was the potent Gloster Javelin – a far cry from the Camels with which it pioneered its night fighting techniques.

The RAF's day bomber squadrons, meanwhile, continued to attack their objectives

Above: Bristol F 2Bs of No 141 (Home Defence) Squadron at Biggin Hill, 1918.

through stiff opposition. On 10 June, for example, Captain George Fox-Rule and Lt E.H. Tredcroft of No 49 Squadron, Fourneuil, were carrying out a low-level bombing attack in their DH 4 when they were jumped by five Albatros Scouts which cut off their line of escape. Fox-Rule promptly dived through the middle of the enemy formation and fired a long burst into the leader, which burst into flames and was seen to hit the ground. The DH 4 was then attacked by three more enemy fighters, which came in from astern. Tredcroft opened fire, sending one down out of control and forcing the others to break off. Fox-Rule brought his aircraft safely back, although its tailplane bracing wires had been shot through.

In another incident on the same day, Lt C.W. Peckham and Sgt J. Grant of No 57 Squadron were carrying out a daylight bombing attack on an ammunition dump at Bapaume when they were attacked by eight Fokker Triplanes. Grant fired at the first one, which went down in flames. The others then positioned themselves west of the DH 4, forcing Peckham to fly north; one of them broke away and opened fire from beneath the bomber, but Peckham turned swiftly and dived on his attacker, firing eighty rounds into it from his front gun. It, too, went down in flames and the rest broke off the action, enabling the DH 4 to make its escape.

On 17 June, the crew of a No 205 Squadron DH 4 from Bois de Roche had a very lucky escape when, during an attack on Chaulnes, the pilot – Captain Gamon – was hit in the head by shrapnel from an anti-aircraft burst, and fainted. More shrapnel struck the engine, severing the main fuel pipe, and a fire broke out. The DH 4 went out of control and spiralled down for 1,000 feet; the fire went out and the observer, Major Goble, managed to bring the aircraft under control. He released his bombs and turned towards the lines, the DH 4 gliding over them at 6,000 feet. At this point the pilot regained consciousness and took control again, just in time

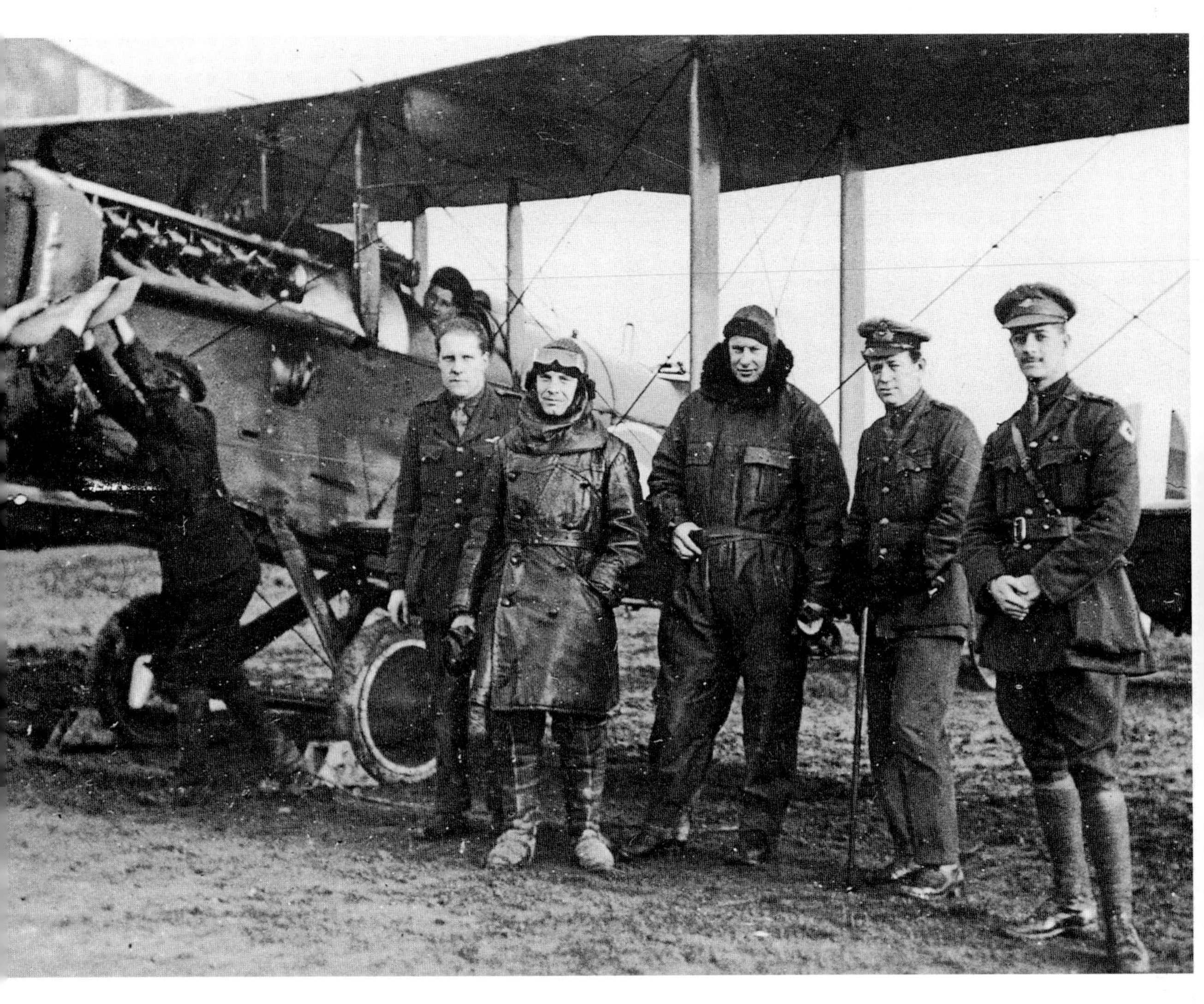

Above: DH 4 and personnel of No 5 (Naval) Squadron, early 1918.

to take evasive action and shake off a Pfalz Scout which made several determined attacks on the aircraft. He landed safely a few minutes later.

It was a gunner of No 205 Squadron – Airman 1st Class (later Sergeant) W.J. Middleton – who was awarded the first Distinguished Flying Medal. The Distinguished Flying Cross and Air Force Cross for officers, and the Distinguished Flying Medal and Air Force Medal for other ranks, were introduced on 3 June 1918; thirty-one DFCs had been awarded by the end of the

Right: Formation of DH 9 day bombers.

Above: The Airco DH 9 was an initial disappointment, having a performance inferior to that of the DH 4, the aircraft it was supposed to replace.

month. The apparent class distinction of awarding different medals for equal acts of gallantry was following the precedent set by the Military Cross and Military Medal, and it is doubtful whether anyone thought much about it at the time; but it was to be nearly eighty years before the distinction was eliminated.

June 1918 saw the formation of the Independent Force RAF, commanded by Major-General Sir Hugh Trenchard. It was the first aerial force in the world to be formed for the purpose of conducting a strategic war against the enemy without reference or subordination to either the Army or Navy, and was the ancestor of RAF Bomber Command. The Independent Force comprised the squadrons of the former VIII Brigade, from which it was formed. Some new units had been added to its strength in May; these were Nos 99 and 104 Squadrons, both fresh out from England and equipped with DH 9s.

Derived from the DH 4, the DH 9 had first entered service with No 103 Squadron at Old Sarum, Wiltshire, in December 1917, and had first gone into action with No 6 Squadron in France the following March. Crews had soon discovered that the DH 9 had a disappointing performance, mainly because its BHP engine and derivatives yielded only 230 hp instead of the anticipated 300. With a full bomb load the DH 9 could barely climb to 15,000 feet, which was 7,000 feet lower than the ceiling of the DH 4, which it was supposed to replace. In addition, fuel consumption above 10,000 feet was appallingly high at fifteen gallons per hour, and engine failures were rife; of twelve DH 9s which set out to bomb the railway triangle at Metz-Sablon on 29 May, for example, six were forced to turn back with engine trouble.

Although the Independent Force had a strategic task, sixty-three per cent of its sorties in

Above: The Breguet 14 was the mainstay of the French and USAS bomber forces. Many examples were used commercially after the war.

June 1918 were flown against tactical targets such as rail complexes and airfields, the remaining twenty-seven per cent being flown against either the German chemical industry or the iron and steel industry. In all, seventy-seven raids were carried out during the month.

The French also formed a strategic bombing force in May 1918, although this remained subordinate to the Army, and like the Independent Force RAF much of its effort was devoted to attacks on tactical objectives. In January 1918 the French day bomber force, which was equipped with the excellent Breguet 14, had undergone a complete transformation, being organized into two fighting groups, each with the same structure. The first, known as the *Groupement Menard*, comprised *Escadre de Combat* 1 and *Escadre de Bombardement* 2; the former consisted of GC 15, 18 and 19, each with four *Escadrilles* of eighteen fighters (SPAD VII or XIII), while the latter had three bomber groups, GB 5, 6 and 9, each with three *Escadrilles* of Breguets.

The other fighting group, the *Groupement Féquant*, comprised *Escadre de Combat* 2 with GC 11, 13 and 17, and *Escadre de Bombardement* 13 with two bomber groups, GB 3 and 4. By May 1918, both fighting groups had a collective total of fifty Breguet 14 day bombers and 130 fighters, the latter having the task of escorting the bombers to and from their objectives.

In that month, both fighting groups were united under the newly-created 1st Air Division, commanded by General Duval. Night bombing was undertaken by GB 1 and 2, also equipped with Breguets, and these units undertook a number of operations against industrial objectives in the Saar during the summer months of 1918. The day bomber units, on the other hand, acted mainly in the support role, carrying out missions to a maximum depth of about twenty miles into enemy territory.

With the formation of the 1st Air Division, the

French began to experiment with very large attack formations, two *Groupes de Chasse* usually being assigned to escort one *Escadre de Bombardement*. Difficulties at once arose: the SPAD fighters were poorly suited to close escort work, which restricted their traditional freedom of action, and they found trouble in making rendezvous with bombers at the appointed time. Another tactic employed involved the fighters sweeping ahead of the bombers to draw enemy fighters on to themselves; having disposed of the opposition, the French fighters would then rendezvous with the bombers and escort them away from the target after they had bombed. The disadvantage here was that the bombers were left unescorted during the most dangerous part of their mission.

With these snags in mind, the French tended to adopt the close escort technique whenever possible, this being judged the lesser of two evils. The result was a large, unmanageable formation. On 16 May, for example, twenty-three Breguets of GB 9 set out on a raid preceded by thirty-six SPADS of GC 18 and followed by twenty-three more of GC 11. The whole armada trailed across five miles of sky, and when it was subjected to determined attacks by small numbers of German fighters the French aircraft simply got in each others' way and got the worst of the encounter. Years later, the Germans were to have the same experience when their fighters were tied to close escort in the Battle of Britain. The RAF adopted different and much more successful tactics when day bomber escorts were

Below: The Farman F 40 bomber-reconnaissance aircraft served with 47 *Escadrilles* on the Western Front and in Macedonia. It was relegated to the training role in 1918.

Above: Handley Page O/400 on a sortie.

Above: Handley Page O/400. This particular example belongs to No 1 School of Navigation and Bomb Dropping, Stonehenge.

called for; the latter were usually carried out at squadron strength, or even less, and the British fighters would fly several thousand feet higher than the bombers in the hope of 'bouncing' the enemy once the latter had committed themselves. These tactics usually worked; but the French refused to learn, and persisted with close escort to the bitter end.

On 4 July 1918 the Independent Force's striking power was augmented by the arrival in France of No 215 Squadron, equipped with the Handley Page O/400 night bomber. After some weeks at Alquines, the squadron moved to Xaffevillers on 19 August. Another O/400 squadron, No 97, was already installed there, having flown over from England on 9 August; a third O/400 unit, No 115 Squadron, was to follow on 1 September, being based at Roville-sur-Chenes.

A development of the O/100, the O/400 was powered by two 360 hp Rolls-Royce Eagle engines, which gave it a maximum speed of 95 mph and an operational ceiling of 8,500 feet. Its maximum endurance was around eight hours. Defensive armament comprised one or two Lewis guns mounted in both nose and rear cockpits; in the latter position one gun was fired sideways or backwards from a raised platform while the second could be fired downwards through a trapdoor in the fuselage floor. The O/400 carried a maximum bomb load of 2,000 lb and was fitted with a new bombsight designed by Lieutenant-Commander Wimperis; the Drift Sight Mk 1A took account of the aircraft's height above the target, its airspeed, wind velocity and drift. It was far from efficient, but it was a vast improvement on the rudimentary equipment used previously.

The arrival of this new type enabled the Independent Force to step up its night bombing effort. The DH 9s, however, were still heavily committed to day bombing missions against

Below: Handley Page O/100 of No 100 Sqn at Xaffevillers, 1918.

strategic targets and took increasingly heavy punishment, especially since the potent Siemens-Schuckert D III fighter had now returned to operational service after undergoing modifications. It equipped *Jasta*s 4a, 4b, 5, 6 and 8, all assigned to the defence of German industrial targets.

At 7.30 am on 22 August, thirteen DH 9s of No 104 Squadron set out from Azelot in two formations of six and seven aircraft to bomb the Badische Anilin factory at Mannheim (a key target, as it produced a high proportion of Germany's explosives). One aircraft in the rear flight turned back over the lines with engine trouble, and soon afterwards another was shot down by heavy anti-aircraft fire. Then the fire died away as eight enemy scouts appeared; they remained on the flanks of the formation, waiting to pick off stragglers and contenting themselves with exchanging a few shots at long range. Their chance came when the DH 9 flown by Lt J. Valentine suffered engine failure; they pounced on him as he broke formation and glided down, but he survived intense attacks to make a forced landing behind the enemy lines. Over the Vosges mountains a third DH 9, piloted by Captain McKay, 'B' Flight commander, also had engine failure and had to come down, the crew being taken prisoner.

The remaining DH 9s approached Mannheim at 11,500 feet. As they started their bombing run they were attacked by fifteen Fokker and Pfalz Scouts, SSW D IIIs and Halberstadt two-seaters. In the ensuing battle the RAF formation was broken up and forced down to 6,000 feet, where two of the scattered bombers were quickly shot down. The five surviving aircraft managed to fight their way back to base, but it had been a black day for the squadron, which had lost seven out of twelve DH 9s and most of its best aircrew.

Yet the DH 9 was capable of giving an excellent account of itself. On 23 August, an aircraft of No 49 Squadron, returning from a bombing raid and crewed by Lt A.R. Spurling and Sgt F.W. Bell, became separated from the rest of the formation in cloud. After flying west for some time, Spurling saw what he took to be a friendly airfield and prepared to land, but as he lost height he was suddenly attacked by a Fokker D VII. Spurling then saw a formation of thirty more Fokkers directly below him and, with little other option, continued his dive through the middle of them, firing as he went. One of the Fokkers was hit and burst into flames; two more, taking violent evasive action, went into a spin and one of them was seen to crash. The DH 9 was then harried from astern by four Fokkers, one of which was shot down in flames by Sgt Bell; a few moments later Bell also accounted for another which attempted a beam attack. The DH 9 was pursued by three more D VIIs as it climbed hard towards the lines, but they did not attack. An enemy two-seater tried to intercept it as it headed for home, but a few well-aimed bursts from Bell drove it away. The fact that Spurling was awarded the DFC and Bell the DFM came as no surprise to their squadron colleagues.

The Independent Force carried out a particularly effective bombing attack on the night of 25/26 August, when two O/400s of No 215 Squadron set out from Xaffervilliers to attack the Badische Anilin Works at Mannheim. The plan was well co-ordinated, and called for the first aircraft, flown by Captain W.B. Lawson, to approach Mannheim at 5,000 feet and draw the enemy fire. As soon as he was joined by the second O/400, flown by Lt M.C. Purvis, Lawson was to leave the target area and shut down his engines, gliding back from a distance of four miles, which was calculated to bring him over the target at 1,000 feet. In fact, Lawson mistimed his glide and arrived over the factory at 200 feet, the aircraft bucking wildly in the explosions of its own bombs. By this time the whole target area was brightly lit by enemy searchlights, probing for the low-flying bomber, and the crew had no difficulty in finding objectives for their

Above: Handley Page O/100 3134. This aircraft was shot down on the night of 22/23 May 1918.

load of 20 lb Cooper bombs. Lawson remained over the target for seven minutes, strafing the factory and searchlight batteries, then Purvis came in to bomb and strafe from the slightly safer altitude of 400 feet. A section of the works was put out of action for a fortnight, but the damage was limited by the failure of many of the bombs to explode.

Meanwhile, following the failure of the German spring offensive, there had been a renewal of trench warfare on the Western Front. This time, it was not to last.

Left: Types of German bomb. The aircraft in the background is a DFW C V.

CHAPTER ELEVEN

Battlefield support, summer 1918

The resumption of trench warfare in the early summer of 1918 made particularly heavy demands on the observation squadrons of both sides, for there were entirely new trench systems to be registered and artillery emplacements to be pinpointed. The RE 8s of No 3 Squadron, Australian Flying Corps, were particularly effective during this period, although they suffered heavily in the process. Occasionally, however, the Australians were able to get their own back. On 6 June, No 3 Squadron aircraft directed some very accurate counter-battery fire on to enemy artillery positions entrenched in the woods between Sailly Laurette and Etinahem, silencing eight of them. A further nine batteries were knocked out the next day. On 10 June, during another counter-battery sortie, Lts R.C. Armstrong and F.J. Hart were returning to base when they noticed anti-aircraft fire near Querrieu. Armstrong flew towards the shell bursts to investigate, and sighted a lone Halberstadt at 2,000 feet, heading east. They cut across its route and, to their astonishment, found that the German crew had no inclination to fight; they made only a feeble attempt to get away, and the Australians were able to shepherd the enemy aircraft without difficulty to Flesselles, where it made a good landing. It was something of a coup, for documents found on the captured Germans, including detailed maps, gave the order of battle of the German forces deployed against the French on the Noyon front.

Below: The DFW C V, one of the finest German observation aircraft.

Observation activities were constantly hampered by poor weather, the problems multiplying when reconnaissances were flown at night. The RAF operations summary for 15 June 1918 records that

'Three machines of 83 Squadron left at 11.5 pm, 11.10 pm and 11.12 pm to carry out a reconnaissance of the area Cambrai–Le Cateau–St Quentin–Peronne. All machines had to be sent together as a clear interval occurred in the weather at 11 pm. The machines returned respectively at 1.5 am, 1.10 am and 2.12 am. Reconnaissances were carried out from heights varying from 800 to 2,500 feet, but were greatly hindered owing to severe rain storms and low clouds. Several Michelin flares were dropped; a number of lights were seen in woods west of Estrees, and a considerable amount of transport was observed on the road at the SW edge of Manancourt Wood. Another column of transport was seen on the main road three miles west of Cambrai proceeding in the direction of Bapaume. Observation in the majority of cases was rendered very difficult owing to machines having to alter their altitude very frequently through running into banks of clouds.'

On 27 June, No 3 Squadron carried out extensive photo-coverage of the Hamel area. They also pioneered a technique which was to prove of enormous value in future operations: the dropping by parachute of small arms ammunition to Allied troops in newly-captured positions, saving the infantry a lot of effort and risk. Using information gleaned from a captured enemy document, the bomb racks of the RE 8s were fitted with clips to hold two boxes each containing 2,000 rounds of .303 ammunition, above which were metal canisters for the packed parachutes. The latter were made of aeroplane fabric, with a fourteen-foot diameter and a one-foot hole at the top. The observer released the boxes by means of a Bowden cable and their weight pulled the parachutes from the canisters.

Trial drops were made in June by No 3 Squadron's Captain L.J Wackett, and were so successful that the technique was quickly adopted by the RAF's army co-operation squadrons. On 4 July, No 9 Squadron RAF, operating from Flesselles, was detailed to drop ammunition to forward troops of the 4th Australian Division east of Nieppe. As the advance developed the troops marked the main dropping points with a white 'N', while individual machine-gun posts requiring ammunition displayed the letter 'V'.

The operation was carried out in close co-operation with No 3 Squadron. Just before dawn on the 4th, the whole squadron flew low over Hamel, dropping bombs and generally making as much noise as possible to cover the sounds of the advancing Australian Corps. The attack was over in a short time, with remarkably light casualties, and in mid-morning No 9 Squadron began its supply-dropping activities, Major J.R. Rodwell's twelve RE 8s averaging four thirty-minute sorties to drop ninety-three boxes totalling 111,600 rounds on six aiming points. Refuelling and reloading – the latter carried out by a specially-trained team of sixteen men – had averaged twenty minutes. Eight of the REs had supplied the main positions, while the other four had assisted the machine-gunners. The average dropping height was 200 feet.

Above and following photograph: The Halberstadt CL II ground attack aircraft equipped a number of German *Schlachtstaffeln* in 1918.

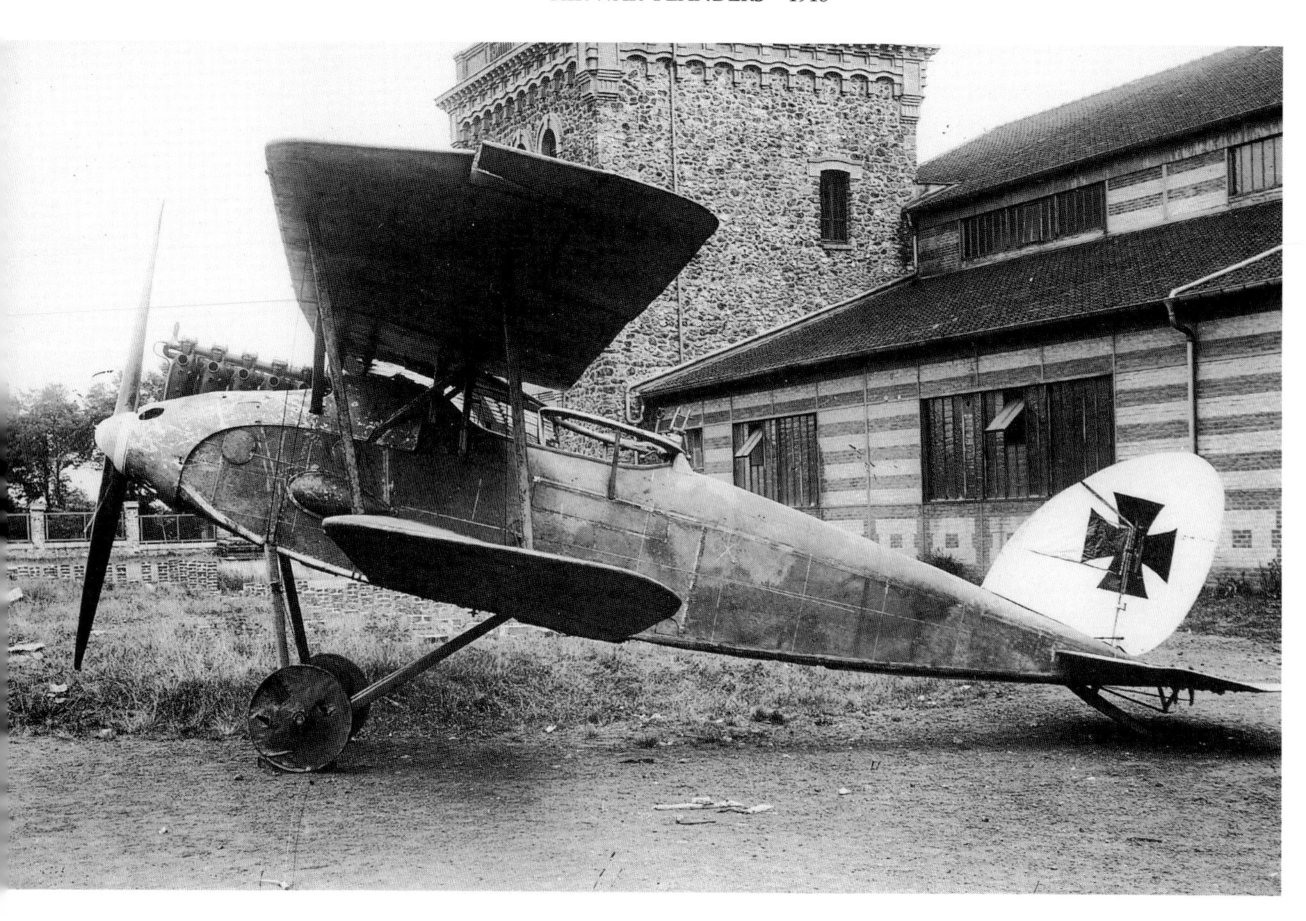

Inevitably, there had been a cost. Two of the low-flying REs, braving intense enemy machine gun fire to deliver their loads, were shot down and their crews killed. They had begun a tradition which was to reach its highest and most tragic hour of gallantry over a quarter of a century later, at Arnhem.

A German observer, *Lt Freiherr* von Pechmann – who was awarded the *Pour le Mérite* – has provided a graphic account of a sortie into British-held territory in June 1918.

> 'One wonderful June morning, when the sky was cloudless and the atmosphere unusually clear, I set out at 6 am to register a shoot for one light and one heavy field battery, and also a 15-cm gun. Archie bursts in the west were thickly dotted together . . . We flew over the region of the Somme battle of 1916, a region which had been beaten and obliterated by the hammerblows of the war god. Here, where once men had lived, there was not a ruin nor a tree to be seen. Only the sad multitudinous piles of rubbish faintly commemorated the sites of former habitations. On our way to Albert we flew over Bouchavesnes, Maurepas, and Maricourt.
>
> 'An English squadron of eigheen D.H.9s flew over us at a great height, turned south, closely followed by our anti-aircraft fire, and dropped their belated Easter eggs on Cappy-sur-Somme, thereby enveloping that small village and its neighbouring aerodrome in thick clouds of smoke. According to official information and instructions, it was necessary to keep a sharp eye on all aircraft, in order to distinguish between friend and foe, and to avoid being taken by surprise.
>
> 'The dump at Becourt-Becordel had for a long time been marked on the map as 'Target No 1, awaiting registration,' and it was decided that a

shoot could also be carried out on the sugar factory at Ribemont. In that position there was a battery which had bombarded the bridges over the Ancre, and had harried the progress of the morning rations to the troops in the front line. A slight pressure on the key of the wireless apparatus, and the four guns of my battery flashed in a small wood. Forty seconds later four shells burst in the garden to the east of the factory, some 200 yards short. The hostile battery, wishing to conceal its whereabouts, ceased fire, but we were not to be deceived by any such clumsy artifice. Two minutes later the next salvo placed two shells on the factory and two close by. After a bombardment lasting half an hour, the factory went up in flames, and the explosion of ammunition informed us that our friends, the Tommies, had stored all sorts of useful materiel on the spot. We were busy registering on our first target when from the west approached five hideous machines, dirty green in colour and ornamented with tricolour circles, but, on seeing the triplanes that were hovering over us, they came to the conclusion that we had better be left in peace . . .

'Next we went to our second target, a battery emplaced on the southern outskirts of Bresle, and proceeded to bombard them. This was paying them back in their own coinage, for we interrupted them in the process of shelling our own battery. The work seemed to last so long that we began to be anxious concerning our supply of petrol, for we still had a third battery marked on our map as being ready to receive our attention.

'After two hours, however, we had finished with our second target, and signals were laid out on the

Below: The Halberstadt CL IV was an improved, more manoeuvrable version of the CL II.

ground to notify us that we should now register on Target No 3. This was the most important and also the most difficult target, namely the ammunition dump just to the east of Warloy. Unfortunately, at that moment, a formation of Albatros took the place of the Triplanes; consequently the abhorred Sopwiths endeavoured to surprise us by diving out of the sun. Before we could get to work with our machine-guns we were twice driven away from the front far back behind our own lines . . . then the Albatros scouts took on these gentlemen, and soon one was punished for his audacity, going down in flames. The others, easily frightened, flew back over the lines, and I was able to continue my work.

'The first shot fell right into the middle of Warloy, and caused a mechanical transport column which was standing by the roadside to retreat from the village along the road to the east with great rapidity. That pleased me well enough, for we could follow them up with our shells. The next burst, although, indeed, 550 yards short with respect to the ammunition dump, threw up a great cloud of smoke and dust only 120 yards from the routed column . . . It was not possible for the troops to make any cover afforded by any dug-out, and their retreat was also cut off. They therefore left the lorries to look after themselves, and presumably retired to a place of safety.

'I kept my position under the Albatros formation, and, feeling now perfectly secure, amused myself with the binoculars, endeavouring to discover what had actually become of the column. After observing the fifth shell burst, I was very unceremoniously aroused from my interesting occupation by the sudden rattle of a machine-gun in my immediate neighbourhood. In a flash the rear gun was swung round towards this new aggressor; I had to save my skin from the attentions of two Sopwiths, which were blazing away like the very deuce less than 100 yards away. The radiator of our engine was riddled with bullets, and the water spurted past our faces as we went down in the tightest possible spiral, with the wires screaming and wailing. It was only thanks to the skilful flying of my pilot that we did not obey the summons to a better world, very much the worse for a few dozen bullet holes, for the two Englishmen, with their four machine-guns, could out-manoeuvre us every time, and so the odds were greatly against us. Our spiral was so steep that I actually thought that our machine was out of control, and that the pilot was badly wounded. There was no time, however, for fears of that sort; we had got to escape, that was clear. We were then only 150 feet or so over Albert, but the pestering fellows would not leave us, and so we had to work our way still farther east.

'But the good old engine could not endure being without water any longer, and it was clear that we should have to land among the shell-holes. Then at last our uninvited escort left us to our own devices, and went off to scrape an acquaintance with an observation balloon. Their advances, however, were not well received in that quarter. Finally, when we had reached Montauban, the engine gave out altogether. There was no time to select a landing ground, for our height was only 150 feet, and, in any case, each shell-hole bordered on its neighbour. My pilot let the machine glide as far as possible, and then, with only 15 yards of clear ground to land on, put the old L.V.G. down without a wire being strained, a few yards from a deep crater among the ruins of Montauban. Before assistance came and we were able to leave that place, we had the satisfaction of seeing one of our late adversaries come to grief in the distance among the smoke clouds of the sugar factory at Ribemont. Two days later my L.V.G., with a new engine, was flying arrogantly again over the ruins of Montauban.'

(Neumann)

One combat that took place in the summer months of 1918 exemplified the courage displayed by the observation crews. In August, with the battle for Amiens in full swing, the RAF's reconnaissance aircraft worked as hard as, if not harder than, they had ever done. Losses were high, and many crews were lucky to escape with their lives as they operated at low level in search of the enemy. One such crew consisted of Captain Ferdinand West – known to everyone as Freddie – and his observer, Lt John Haslam; on 8 and 9 August they made two reconnaissance flights in an Armstrong-Whitworth FK 8 of No 8 Squadron, Vignacourt, and each time their aircraft was so badly damaged by ground fire that they had to crash-land, escaping with no more than shock and a few bruises.

The next day they were sent out again on another reconnaissance, keeping an eye open for the enemy fighters that were reported to be very active over the battlefront. Freddie West was not complacent about them, but neither did he fear them unduly; the 'Big Ack' was a tough nut to crack, and he had developed his own tactics to counter the enemy's, as he explained:

> 'They invariably followed the same tactics. Once they spotted you they went up to about five or six hundred feet above you and then they tried to dive on you, all guns blazing, and shoot you down. Our way to answer was that the observer should open fire immediately he saw the German pilot put his nose down. Often the pilots didn't like being fired at; they broke combat. Occasionally, you had a tougher fellow who wanted to go on fighting. In that case I would try to do a very unpleasant flat turn and try to face the direction the enemy was coming from, because that compelled him to do large turns to the left or to the right and give my observer a chance to fire on him. That's the way we tried to save ourselves.'

On this particular August day, the task of West and Haslam was to locate the enemy's reserves near Amiens, a job that involved flying at 1,500 feet over enemy territory. West described what happened subsequently.

> 'I was lucky, or unlucky, whichever way you want to look at it, and I was delighted to find at last an area where I saw many German troops, a large amount of transport, a large amount of guns – and I thought, this is the information that the army needs. And so, having got this information, I made straight for my aerodrome. Unfortunately, German fighters were also of the opinion that I should not bring back this information, and so I was attacked. During one fight I received some explosive bullets in my left leg, which was almost severed, but you know when you are young you are an optimist, and

Below: LVG C Vs at a forward German airfield.

I think the combination of youth, health and optimism got me back. I am also grateful to my observer who did first-class work with his Lewis guns and I'm glad to have this opportunity to pay a tribute to him, because he is still alive. He became a group captain and a parson. He's a reverend, probably due to my bad language in the aeroplane.'

What West, with typical modesty, does not say in this account – written in the late 1970s – is that he was attacked by seven enemy aircraft, and that despite being wounded in the foot, and his aircraft damaged, he made another circuit of the area to make sure of the enemy dispositions. On the way back to base he came under continual attack, and his virtually severed left leg fell among the controls. He lifted it clear and twisted his clothing into a touniquet with one hand, flying the aircraft with the other, and managed to land on a patch of grass close to some Canadian positions. Desperately weak from loss of blood, he insisted on making his report before being taken to hospital, where his leg was amputated. Haslam was also wounded in the ankle, but not seriously.

Freddie West was later awarded the Victoria Cross, while John Haslam, who already had the DSC for an action in May, now added the DFC to it. After the war, West, fitted with an artificial leg, resigned himself to a legal career, but with the help of Sir Hugh Trenchard he came back into the RAF and regained his flying category. He served as air attaché in Finland, Estonia and Latvia, and on the outbreak of the 1939–45 war he was a station commander in No 2 Group, RAF Bomber Command, with the rank of group captain. He subsequently served on clandestine duties in Switzerland, where he was involved with the RAF's 'escape line', and eventually retired as an air commodore.

If the job of the observation crews was perilous, the task of the balloon observers along the front was equally so, even though they had the advantage of heavy defences to protect them and parachutes to use if the defences failed. Mostly the parachutes worked, but sometimes they did not, as Lt Smith of No 29 Balloon Section found to his cost on 19 June 1918. With Flight Sergeant Shepherd – who was seriously wounded in the back during the attack – he took to his parachute after their balloon was set on fire by an enemy aircraft. Shepherd's parachute opened but Smith's did not. He fell for several hundred feet, crashed through the branches of a tree and fell into a bog, from which he emerged with no more than a severe shaking.

Chapter Twelve
American eagles

The formal involvement of the United States Army in France began on 15 January 1918, with the formation at Neufchateau of the US 1st Army Corps, comprising the 1st, 2nd, 26th and 42nd Divisions under General Liggett. The troops, a mixture of conscripts and volunteers, were untrained and poorly equipped, and it would be several months before they were ready to go into the line.

In the early weeks of 1918 the Americans were even more ill-fitted to contribute to the air war in France than they were to take part in the land campaign. In 1917, American military air power, such as it was, was embodied in the Aviation Section of the US Signal Corps; its inventory of less than 300 aircraft did not include a single combat machine. Numerically, the most important type in service was the Curtiss JN4 trainer, known as the 'Jenny', which also served in a training capacity with the RFC and RNAS.

Following America's entry into the war, with a resulting massive increase in the budget available to expand the country's military aviation resources, the US Army sent Colonel Raynal C. Bolling to Europe to make a first-hand assessment of the type of equipment that would be needed by the American air units joining the Allied forces. Bolling found American volunteer pilots flying British and French aircraft that were already far superior to anything the embryo American aviation industry could design and produce in the limited time available, and so it was decided that the Americans would concentrate on building training and reconnaissance aircraft while their future combat pilots flew Nieuports and SPADS.

The nucleus of those combat pilots, and a highly experienced one at that, already existed. American volunteers had been serving with the *Aéronautique Militaire* since 1915, having arrived via the French Foreign Legion, which had granted them French citizenship for the duration of their military service and therefore neatly avoided any possible political complications. In the autumn of 1915, the idea of banding all the Americans together in one squadron had been nurtured by Edmund L. Gros, a doctor of medicine who had already helped to form an American Ambulance Service in France during the early months of the war. The original idea was not that of Gros, but of a young pilot named Norman Prince, of Pride's Crossing in Massachusetts, who came to Paris, teamed up with the doctor and started a recruiting campaign to comb the Foreign Legion, the Ambulance Service and the French forces in search of Americans who might be willing to volunteer for flying duties. As soon as a likely candidate was located, and showed willing, Gros had him transferred to the *Aéronautique Militaire* for training; this step was accomplished with the help of Jarousse de Silac, a senior member of the French war ministry, who believed that it was only a matter of time before America entered the war on the Allied side anyway.

As soon as the American airmen completed their training they were posted to various air units for operational service, while Gros and his colleagues worked hard behind the scenes to obtain official approval for the formation of an

American squadron. The word spread quickly and more volunteers began to arrive from the United States, some of them having tried to join the RFC. In the spring of 1916 they were all either operational or under training in France, awaiting the call from Gros and Prince.

It came on 17 April 1916. On that day the *Escadrille Américaine* – known officially as *Escadrille* N.124 – was formed around a nucleus of seven pilots, with Norman Prince at their head. During the next few days seven more arrived, having been detached from their respective French units. Among them was one Gervais Raoul Victor Lufbery, who had been one of the first to enlist in 1914.

The son of an American father and a French mother, Lufbery had spent his childhood in Willingford, Connecticut, and had quickly developed a taste for adventure. At the age of seventeen he had set off to see the world, visiting France, North Africa, the Balkans, Germany and South America. Returning home, he joined the US Army at the age of eighteen, spending most of his two-year period of service in the Philippines, then set out to travel the world again, this time heading for the Far East.

In 1912, in Saigon, he met a French pilot named Marc Pourpe. Like Lufbery, Pourpe was an adventurer; he had learned to fly, bought himself one of Henri Farman's early biplanes, and set off on a world tour with it, giving flying lessons and joyrides to anyone willing to pay for the privilege. Lufbery was fascinated by this flamboyant character and the two became good friends, the American volunteering to be Pourpe's mechanic. Before long Lufbery too had learned to fly, and for the next couple of years the two travelled through India, China and Japan, giving flying demonstrations. Early in 1914 they went to Egypt, and Pourpe made history by carrying out a record non-stop flight from Cairo to Khartoum.

By this time the Farman was practically worn out, so in the summer of 1914 the pair went to France with the intention of buying a new one. They were still there in August, when France and Germany went to war.

Pourpe at once enlisted in the *Aéronautique Militaire*, where his flying skills would be put to good use. Lufbery wanted to do the same, but his American citizenship proved an obstacle. He quickly found the Foreign Legion loophole and joined up, automatically becoming a French citizen for the duration of his service, and soon afterwards he applied for a transfer to the air arm. He put in a request to be Pourpe's mechanic, and to his delight it was granted.

When Pourpe was killed in December 1914, Raoul Lufbery volunteered for flying duties. His early military flying career was far from spectacular; in fact, his performance indicated that he was not suited to handling light and manoeuvrable aircraft such as single-seat scouts, and his instructors said that he lacked the necessary finesse to become a really proficient pilot. He completed the flying course and was awarded his wings, but to his disappointment he was posted to a bomber unit, VB.102, flying Voisin biplanes. He was still there in May 1916, when Gros and Prince came to his rescue and engineered his transfer to N.124.

The *Escadrille*, which was equipped with Nieuport Scouts, moved up to Bar-le-Duc, in the Verdun sector, and its pilots – many of whom, like Lufbery, had already acquired considerable experience with the French – soon began to distinguish themselves. During the next five months they took part in 156 air combats and officially destroyed seventeen enemy aircraft. The first to score was Lieutenant Kiffin Rockwell, who shot down a two-seater on 18 May, and who destroyed two more enemy aircraft before the end of the year. Norman Prince claimed five victories before he was killed in a night landing accident in October, while Lts Bert Hall and Bill Thaw got two and one respectively. But the rising star of the *Escadrille* was Lufbery, who gained his first victory on 31

Above: USAAS reconnaissance photograph of a German airfield. The aircraft visible to the right of the farmhouse is an all-metal Junkers J 1 army co-operation machine.

July 1916 and whose score had risen to six enemy aircraft destroyed by the end of the year.

Late in 1916 the *Escadrille* moved to the Somme sector. By that time its fighting prowess was so well established that the German Government lodged a protest with the United States against the unit's existence, claiming that the word *Américaine* in its title was a violation of US neutrality. The French Government accordingly decided to change the title to *Escadrille* Lafayette, the name recalling the French soldier and nobleman who had fought for the Americans in the War of Independence. By the end of 1916 the score of the *Escadrille* Lafayette stood at forty-two enemy aircraft destroyed. The leading scorer was Raoul Lufbery, with sixteen, followed by Lts Bill Thaw and de Laage – the latter a Frenchman – with four each.

By the time the United States entered the war in April 1917, the score of the *Escadrille* Lafayette stood at 199 enemy aircraft. Although the American Air Service began to establish itself in France at the beginning of 1918, and although the American airmen already in action were transferred to it on paper, with US Army ranks, there was no speedy transfer of personnel to form new American air units. The Americans had no shortage of manpower, their physical requirements were high, and – incredible though it may seem – some of the men who had fought so well with the *Escadrille* Lafayette were found to be below the required standard.

In January 1918 Raoul Lufbery, who now had sixteen victories to his credit, was commissioned into the US Army with the rank of major, and expected to receive orders to form an American fighter squadron. Instead, to his disgust, he was sent to a training school at Issoudun, where recruits to the Air Service were given basic training before starting their flying courses. It was to be three months before he returned to operational flying.

At last, in April 1918, he was posted to command the 94th Aero (Pursuit) Squadron in the Champagne sector. Together with its sister squadron, the 95th – the latter being the first American fighter squadron to form in France, on 18 February 1918 – this unit made up the American First Pursuit Group. The 94th Squadron was the first to be declared combat-ready, but Lufbery fought a hard battle to bring it to that status. In the middle of April, for example, the squadron's Nieuports still had no guns; it seemed that some supply officer, somewhere far to the rear, deemed the issue of socks more important than the issue of weapons. In the end Lufbery took his case directly to General Pershing, the American Air Service commander, and after that the guns arrived in record time.

On 18 April, three Nieuport Scouts of the 94th Aero Squadron were detailed to carry out the First Pursuit Group's first combat patrol. It was led by Captain David Petersen, with Lts Reed Chambers and Edward Rickenbacker as his wingmen. The patrol was uneventful and the three pilots returned to their airfield. Soon after they had landed, however, two German aircraft were reported in the area. Two more American pilots, Lts Alan Winslow and Douglas Campbell, immediately took off and each shot down an enemy machine – the first air victories credited to an American squadron.

Lufbery's training schedule was not confined to work in the air. He was always available whenever his pilots wanted his advice, and he would spend long hours with them in the evenings, discussing tactics. His method of fighting was much the same as Mannock's; approach with caution and make sure the odds are in your favour before committing yourself. Above all, he told them, keep a cool head. Panic was the pilot's worst enemy. If your aircraft is set on fire, he advised them, side-slip to keep the flames away from the cockpit and get down as quickly as you can. That way, you have at least some chance of survival; you have none at all if you panic and jump clear.

Raoul Lufbery's luck finally ran out on 19 May 1918, five weeks after he had scored his seventeenth and final victory: an Albatros D III, which he shot down on a freelance patrol. During a fight with another Albatros right over the 94th Squadron's airfield at Toul, his Nieuport was hit and set on fire. In full view of the horrified Americans on the ground, it nosed down and was soon enveloped in flames. It was not hard to imagine the agony of the man in the cockpit as he tried to sidelip through the last few hundred feet. Finally, at only 200 feet above the ground, the flames won. The witnesses saw a dark shape detach itself and plummet to the ground.

They found Lufbery's body in a garden, impaled on a fence in the hamlet of Maron. It was thought that he may have been trying to jump into a small river, which flowed a hundred yards or so away. He was buried in a nearby military cemetery, but his body was later removed and laid to rest in the Parc de Garches, near Marnes-la-Coquette, where there stands a monument to the *Escadrille* Lafayette and its dead. In the manual of air fighting, Raoul Lufbery is remembered for the so-called 'Lufbery Circle', a defensive tactic he devised; it involved a simple defensive circle in which the tail of each aircraft was covered by the one behind, so that an enemy trying to attack any individual aircraft would come under fire from the one following. It was still to be in use in Vietnam half a century later, when North Vietnamese MiG-17 pilots were to use it to counter attacks by faster F-4 Phantoms. Its drawback was that it was difficult to maintain for any length of time, because altitude was progressively lost unless the circle was held at full throttle, in which case fuel was consumed at a high rate.

On 24 May 1918, the Air Arm of the US Signal Corps became the United States Army Air Service under the command of Major-General William Kenley, himself a pilot. By July 1918 the American First Pursuit Group in France had been expanded to five squadrons, the 27th, 94th, 95th, 147th and 185th, the latter reserved for night fighting. They were initially equipped with Nieuport 28s, but later exchanged these for SPADs, which could meet the Fokker D VII on much more favourable terms. The American Expeditionary Force's First Observation Group, formed in the summer of 1918, used the Salmson 2A reconnaissance biplane, and eleven squadrons were eventually equipped with it; the US day bomber squadrons, like their French counterparts, used the Breguet 14.

Below: Lt E.R. Cook of the 91st Aero Squadron and his SPAD XIII.

Above: Sopwith F 1 Camels of the 148th Aero Squadron, USAAS, at Petit Synthe near Dunkirk, 6 August 1918. The nearest aircraft, D9516, was lost in action on 26 August, its pilot – Lt G.V. Siebold – being killed.

Although most American pilots gradually remustered into the US squadrons, some elected to stay with the French and British. Foremost among the latter was Captain W.C. Lambert of No 24 Squadron, who was to end the war with twenty-two victories, Captain A.T. Iaccaci of No 20 Squadron (eighteen victories), Lt F.W. Gillet of No 79 Squadron (seventeen victories), Captain H.A. Kuhlberg of No 1 Squadron and Captain O.J. Rose of No 92 Squadron (sixteen victories each.) In addition, two all-American squadrons, the 17th and 148th, were formed in the summer of 1918 and remained part of the RAF for the duration of the war.

The leading scorer among the American pilots who elected to stay with the French *Aviation Militaire* was *Sous-Lieutenant* Frank Baylies. Born in New Bedford, Massachusetts, in September 1895, Baylies was one of the band of American citizens who had found his way into the war by enlisting in the Ambulance Service in 1916. His first combat unit was SPA.73, after which he was transferred to SPA.3 *Cigognes*. He scored his first victory with the unit, as a corporal, on 19 February 1918 and gained two more victories in March, followed by two in April and seven in May. He quickly showed himself to be a daring and fearless pilot who was quite willing to take on an enemy squadron single-handed. The American Army offered him a transfer with the rank of captain but he refused, preferring to remain as an NCO with the *Cigognes*.

Baylies had a narrow escape on 28 March, when an enemy shell struck his aircraft as he was flying at 300 feet four miles behind the German lines. He kept his machine in the air long enough to reach no-man's land and then ran for it, narrowly avoiding capture by German troops who set off in hot pursuit. His luck held until 17 June, when he set out on patrol with two other NCO pilots. They encountered a formation of aircraft which they believed to be Sopwith Camels; it was a fatal error, for they were in fact Fokker D VIIs. After a short battle, Baylies fell in flames behind the enemy lines at Crèvecouer Lassigny; his fellow pilots escaped by the skin of their teeth, their aircraft riddled with holes. Like Lufbery, Baylies was eventually interred at the Lafayette Memorial. His final score was twelve enemy aircraft destroyed, all between 19 February and 31 May 1918.

Two other notable Americans who remained with the *Aviation Militaire* were James A. Connely and Edwin Parsons, both of whom survived the war with eight confirmed victories. Not a great deal is known about Connely except that he had been born in Philadelphia and had joined the French Army by way of the Foreign Legion; his flying service was with SPA.157 and SPA.163, and his victories were gained between April and November 1918. He died in New York in 1944.

Lieutenant Edwin C. Parsons is better documented. Born in 1892 at Holyoke, Massachusetts, he had joined the Ambulance Service in France and obtained his pilot's brevet a year later. He joined SPA.3 in April 1918 and remained with this unit for the duration of the war, gaining his first victory on 4 September and his eighth on 1 October. In 1940, with the rank of lieutenant-commander, he was to be an instructor at the US Naval Air Station Pensacola, Florida, and subsequently to serve on board an aircraft carrier during the Solomons campaign.

Above: First Lt B. Alexander (plt) and 2nd Lt E. McLennen (observer) of the 96th Aero Squadron USAS setting out on a raid from Amanty aerodrome in their Breguet 14B2 on 29 July 1918.

Above: Sopwith Camel of the 148th Aero Squadron USAAS down in no-man's land.

He retired with the rank of rear-admiral; his decorations included the *Croix de Guerre* with eight palm leaves, and he was to be made an officer of the Legion of Honour in 1961. He died in May 1968 and is buried at Arlington National Cemetery, Washington.

Such were the men who pioneered America's entry into the air combat arena of the First World War. But it was during the summer and autumn of 1918, flying with the fighter squadrons of the US Army Air Service, that the American airmen were to make their true mark.

Chapter Thirteen

July 1918: Ludendorff's last fling

By early July 1918, the fighting on the Western Front had devolved into something rather like a game of chess. After the German reverses on the Aisne in June, Ludendorff now waited for the Allied C-in-C, Marshal Foch, to reveal his strength in some other sector, confident that he had preserved sufficient reserves to stand firm in his own battle positions. Despite the fact that the French now had ten field armies in the line, and that there were several weak spots in the German defences at which Foch might have struck, the marshal was in no hurry; he could now afford to wait until there were sufficient American forces in the west to balance the total number of German forces before launching a major offensive. In the meantime, Foch waited for Ludendorff to make the first move.

The US 1st Division had already gone into action in May, capturing the German salient at Catigny, north-west of Montdidier, on the 28th. Two days later the 3rd Division moved into the line in the Château-Thierry sector, followed by the 2nd Division on 2 June. On 10 June the 2nd Division carried part of Belleau Wood, south-west of Château-Thierry, and this initial success was completed in the last week of the month, at considerable cost, by the US Marine Brigade. There was a further American success on 1 July, when the 2nd Division captured Vaux, at the corner of the Marne salient, and took 450

Below: Albatros D Vs of *Jasta* 27.

prisoners. On the 4th, American troops were brigaded with British forces for the first time, and General Monash's Australian Corps, together with US troops of General Bell's 33rd Division, captured Hamel and took over 1,500 prisoners between them. Also on 4 July, an appropriate date in American history, the arrival of more US forces in the line permitted the US First Army Corps to be regrouped; it now comprised the 1st, 2nd, 3rd, 4th, 26th and 28th Divisions.

The first day of July saw some bitter air fighting, with both sides airborne in strength. One of the day's more notable air combats involved Captain J. Gilmour of No 65 Squadron (Sopwith Camels), who encountered a Fokker Triplane while leading his patrol and dived on it, shooting it down in flames. Shortly afterwards he led his patrol in an attack on forty enemy aircraft and engaged an Albatros at point-blank range. Its wings fell off as it went into a steep dive and he turned on another, seeing it go into an upside-down spiral, apparently out of control. By this time his patrol had become scattered, and so Gilmour decided to return to base at Bertangles. As he flew back towards the lines he was attacked by four Albatros Scouts; as their leader closed to within firing range Gilmour neatly reversed the situation by pulling up into an Immelmann turn (a stall turn followed by a half roll, devised by the German ace Max Immelmann in 1915) which placed him on the enemy's tail. Gilmour fired his remaining ammunition into the Albatros, which went down to crash, and then dived for sanctuary.

It was now becoming apparent that the German pilots were generally of a lower standard than the men who had wrought such havoc on the Allied squadrons in 1917. On 1 July, for example, Major E.J. McLaughty of No 4 Squadron AFC thought he had cause for concern when he was attacked by three Pfalz Scouts, only to see two of them collide as they dived on him. He at once engaged the survivor, which broke off the engagement and fled eastwards, then looked for the two that had collided. He saw that one of them had crashed but that the other was descending in a slow spiral, apparently still under control, if only just. In no mood to be chivalrous, the Australian fired 100 rounds into it and sent it down in flames.

Panic among the German pilots was also evident on the following day, when a patrol of five SE 5s of No 60 Squadron, led by Lt A.W. Saunders, sighted a formation of six Pfalz Scouts some 7,000 feet below, flying over Villers Bretonneux. Saunders led the patrol down and attacked the left-hand Pfalz, which went down and crashed after he had fired a drum of Lewis and a long burst of Vickers into it. As soon as he started his attack, the next Pfalz in line suddenly broke hard to the right and collided with the leader. Both aircraft, tangled together, went down and crashed in the Bois de Pierret.

When Ludendorff's expected attack came, it fell upon the French and Americans, and consequently it was their squadrons which bore the brunt of the fighting in mid-July. The last great German offensive of the war began on 15 July on a fifty-mile front to the east and west of Reims, the main German thrust aiming to cross the Marne. The attack was preceded by a bombardment of furious intensity, its thunder awakening the inhabitants of Paris in the early hours of the morning.

The Allied air units were rapidly concentrated to meet the threat. The *Cigognes* were moved to a forward airstrip, Trecon in the Château-Thierry sector, while nine RAF squadrons flew southwards through rainstorms a few hours before the opening of the battle proper. Much of the RAF's effort was devoted to airfield attacks; during the morning, for example, Nos 65 and 209 Squadrons, escorted by Nos 23, 24 and 84 Squadrons, dropped 105 25 lb bombs on Foucaucourt aerodrome and fired 8,300 rounds into the hangars and other buildings in a series of low-level attacks. Many direct hits were obtained, and two hangars set on fire. All the RAF aircraft returned safely, shooting down two enemy balloons on the way back.

Despite damaging attacks such as this, the German Flying Corps operated in strength throughout the offensive, and suffered substantial casualties. JG 1 'Richthofen' was in the area opposite Château-Thierry, and before the month was out it had lost seven of its leading pilots. *Leutnant* Fritz Friedrichs of *Jasta* 10, with twenty-one victories, was shot down and killed on the day the attack started, while *Leutnant* Hans Kirchstein (twenty-seven victories) and *Vizefeldwebel* Fritz Krebs, with six victories, were lost on the following day. Both pilots belonged to *Jasta* 6.

Of all the German aces who survived to see the summer of 1918, one seemed to bear a charmed life. *Leutnant* Ernst Udet had gained his twentieth victory in April and and had been awarded the coveted *Pour le Mérite*; since then his rise had been meteoric. At the head of *Jasta* 4, he and the new Fokker D VII proved a deadly combination, and by the end of the war he was to amass sixty-two kills, making him the top-scoring German pilot after von Richthofen. After the war he went on to achieve international fame as a test, sporting and aerobatic pilot. In 1935 he joined the new *Luftwaffe* and was eventually appointed to the post of Director-General of Equipment. The fact that he had little talent for organization became apparent in the early months of the Russian campaign in 1941, when his department failed to produce aircraft in sufficient numbers to make good the heavy German losses. In continual conflict with both Hitler and Hermann Göring, his former commanding officer in JG 1, he became increasingly depressed and committed suicide on 17 November, 1941.

Another German ace who rose to the highest command in Hitler's *Luftwaffe* was Robert, *Ritter* von Greim, who commanded *Jasta* 34, JG 10, and

Below and the following three photographs: The Pfalz D III, one of the overlooked fighters of WWI, played a large part in retrieving German air superiority in the air battles of 1918.

ended the war with twenty-eight victories. In April 1945, with the *Luftwaffe* tottering to its collapse, he was appointed by Hitler to succeed Göring as its C-in-C. Taken prisoner by the Allies, he committed suicide in June.

One man who was to play a prominent part in shaping the *Luftwaffe* in the years between the wars was Wolfram von Richthofen of *Jasta* 11, the cousin of Manfred. He ended the war with eight victories and, in 1936, commanded the *Kondor* Legion in Spain. This was followed by an appointment as C-in-C *Fliegerkorps* VIII, in which he brought dive-bombing operations with the Junkers Ju 87 *Stuka* to a fine art during the Polish and French campaigns. He successively commanded *Luftflotte* 4 and *Luftflotte* 2, the latter in the Mediterranean Theatre, but he developed a brain tumour and died in July 1945 after being transferred to the reserve at the end of the previous year.

The air battles of July 1918 established René Fonck for all time as France's ace of aces. On the 16th, as he was flying to join the *Cigognes* at Trecon, having just been recalled from leave in Paris, he sighted a pair of LVG two-seaters directly over the lines, with six Fokker D VIIs 1,500 feet higher up. Despite the fact that his SPAD was encumbered by two suitcases and a case of wine, stuffed under his feet in the cockpit, he decided to attack. Ignoring the Fokkers, he made one pass against the two-seaters and sent both of them down in flames. The Fokkers pursued him, bent on revenge, but he out-ran them and made a safe landing at Trecon, his precious bottles intact. During the next three days, Fonck destroyed five more enemy aircraft, bringing his score so far to fifty-six.

Charles Nungesser was now trailing a long way behind Fonck. He gained his fortieth victory on 16 July, but claimed no more that month. He was physically worn out, and a day later the doctors sent him away for a rest. Like so many other pilots in this war, Nungesser suffered from persistent bouts of sickness; much of it was a consequence of nervous strain, but the real culprit was the castor oil used to lubricate the early aero-engines, which was spewed out and inhaled by pilots in considerable quantities. It had a terribly debilitating effect, and many who survived the war continued to suffer from it in later life.

Close behind Nungesser came Georges Madon, who destroyed his thirty-seventh aircraft on 17 July. He might have been justified in claiming three more, because he was instrumental in their destruction, although he never fired a shot at them. Shorty before he claimed his confirmed victim, a two-seater, he sighted three Pfalz Scouts flying in formation near Epernay and dived out of the sun to attack them. Two broke violently towards one another and collided head-on, falling to earth in a cloud of debris, and the third tried to escape by means of a high speed dive, a fatal thing to do in a Pfalz. The resulting structural failure was catastrophic and the aircraft fell apart, its fragments falling over a wide area. The next day, Madon destroyed a Fokker D VII over Main-de-Massignes, a location on the Champagne downs. Its pilot was *Leutnant* Moritz Bretschneider-Bodener, a member of JG.1's *Jasta* 6, who had five aircraft to his credit.

At first, the German offensive of July 1918 went well. The initial advance was rapid; the Germans overwhelmed the first line of defence and then, seeing that most of the French positions were deserted and that resistance ahead was firm, they began to realize that they had been drawn into a trap. On 18 July Marshal Foch launched his counter-stroke on a twenty-seven mile front between Fontenoy and Belleau, west of Château-Thierry. General Mangin's French Tenth Army, which included the 1st and 2nd US Infantry Divisions, penetrated eight miles into the enemy front, taking 5,000 prisoners, while to the south the Franco-American forces under General Degoutte made an advance of three to five miles. Both moves were heavily supported by tanks, 324 of which were engaged in the Tenth Army's sector.

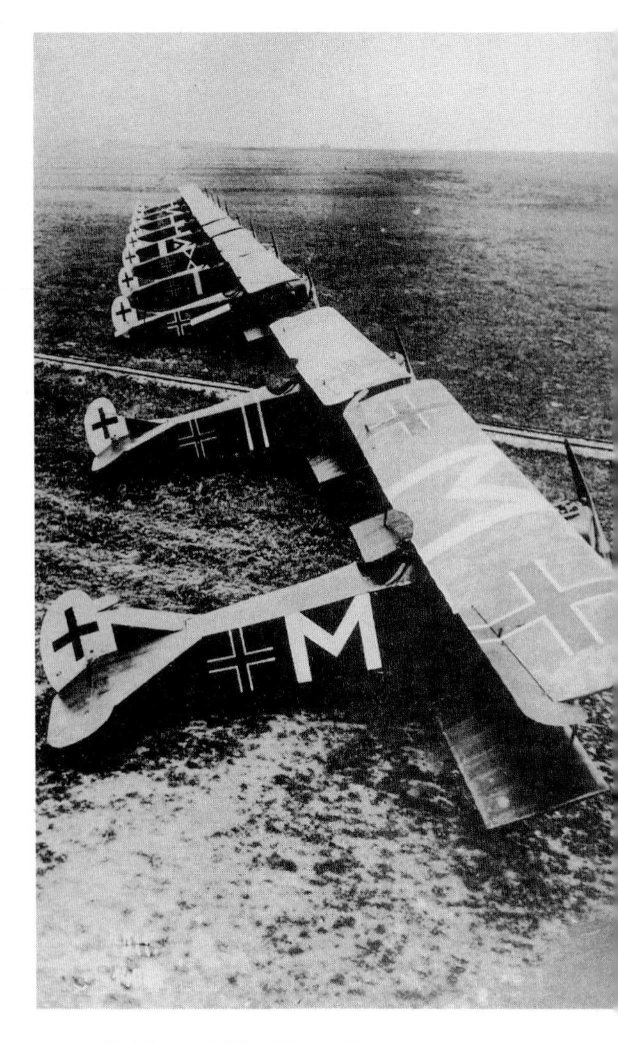

Above: Fokker D VIIs of *Jasta* 72 at Bergnicourt, July 1918.

On 19 July a strong British reserve force arrived to take part in the battle near Reims, going into the line in a sector which had been gallantly defended by Italian troops; the latter had completely destroyed a German division and severely mauled several others. The British force struck along the Ardre river valley at Marfaux, which they won, lost and partly recaptured, and also took Courfon Wood. Strong German forces from the Champagne sector checked the British left but the centre and right fought onward, taking St Euphraise village and Bouilly across the Reims road and threatening the main German communications route running from Fismes and the Ardre valley to the Marne front.

The unexpected British pressure forced the Germans into a rapid retreat across the Marne for the second time in the war. The timely intervention of the British completely disrupted the vast scheme of operations launched by Ludendorff and threw the Germans on the defensive. By a fitting coincidence, it was one of the British formations that had helped to stem the first German assault in March – the Scottish Highland Territorial Division – that now took part in the counter-stroke that threw the enemy into disarray.

As the Germans retreated over the Marne the Franco-American forces closed around Château-Thierry, entering the battered town on 21 July. In the next two days they advanced towards Fère and Oulchy by a southern flanking movement through La Croix, Rocourt and Epieds, cutting the Soissons road in a swaying battle of thrust and counter-thrust that ended, on 28 July, in a magnificent action by the 17th French Division and the 15th Scottish Division, attached to General Mangin's army, who between them stormed and took Grand Rozoy ridge, a critical point in the enemy's defensive line.

Throughout this period of incessant fighting, the Allied air arms maintained pressure on the enemy's airfields, on both the Marne and the Somme. In one spectacular operation on 22 July, Major Raymond Collishaw and Captain L.H. Rochford of No 203 Squadron set out at 3.40 am to attack the aerodrome at Dorignies. Rochford attacked first, firing all his ammunition into the buildings and hangars from 200 feet, and then dropped three Cooper bombs on some barracks and a fourth on a hangar, which went on fire. Collishaw, beginning his run, spotted three aircraft that were being pulled from a hangar and machine-gunned them, after which he dropped four bombs from 150 feet among the barrack huts. Turning, he saw an enemy aircraft approaching to land and attacked it, shooting it down in flames. Two hours later, he returned to survey the damage; three Albatros Scouts which were patrolling the airfield attacked him, but he shot one down and made his escape. Later in the day, Captain Rochford also destroyed a Fokker D VII, and four more – the remainder of the enemy formation – were either shot down or driven down out of control by the other pilots of his patrol, Lts W. Sidebottom and A.E. Rudge.

This period saw the arrival on the Western Front of two RAF fighter squadrons which were to make their mark in the annals of the service. The first was No 92 Squadron which, equipped with SE 5s, arrived at Drionville, south-west of St Omer, on 19 July; three days later its first kill – a Fokker D VII – was scored by one of its flight commanders, Captain J.M. Robb (later Air Marshal Sir James Robb). The other squadron was No 151, whose early night fighting exploits in France have already been mentioned.

On 25 July, Ira Jones of No 74 Squadron flew over to No 85 Squadron's airfield at St Omer to visit his former commanding officer, Mick Mannock. Jones wrote later:

> 'I can't quite make out whether he has got nerves or not. One minute, he's full-out. The next, he gives the impression of being morbid, and keeps bringing up his pet subject of being shot down in flames. I told him I had got a two-seater in flames on patrol this morning before breakfast. 'Could you hear the sod scream?' he asked with a sour smile. 'One day,

Above and the following two photographs: Fokker D VIIs.

they'll get you like that, my lad. You are getting careless. Don't forget to blow your brains out.' Everyone roared with laughter . . .'

Mannock had returned from leave to command No 85 Squadron in the first week of the month, and celebrated his return by shooting down a two-seater on the 8th. At 5.30 on the morning after Jones's visit, Mannock was patrolling the front line at 5,000 feet over Merville, accmpanied by Lt D.C. Inglis – a young New Zealander from Canterbury, as yet unblooded in action – when he sighted a Junkers CL 1 two-seater, an angular, all-metal low-wing monoplane which was just beginning to enter service with the German ground attack squadrons. Mannock, after pointing it out to Inglis, led the New Zealander down to attack, diving and then climbing up under the Junkers' tail. The German aircraft soon caught fire and spun down to crash.

Mannock, contrary to his usual practice, followed it down, firing as it fell. He and Inglis strafed the wreck as it lay burning on the ground, then flew at low level – no higher than 200 feet – towards no-man's land, zig-zagging as they went to avoid the intense small-arms fire that was being directed at them from the enemy positions. Suddenly, near Colonne, Inglis saw the nose of Mannock's SE 5 dip. The left wing dropped slowly, and now Inglis could see a small flicker of flame and a ribbon of smoke coming from the aircraft's starboard side. The SE went into a spin and crashed among some trenches, bursting into flames on impact. Distraught, Inglis braved enemy fire to circle the wreckage several times, but there was no hope that Mannock might have survived. The New Zealander's own aircraft was hit and crash-landed five yards behind the British line; Inglis took cover in a shell crater and was rescued by some Welsh troops, who pulled him into their trench.

Inglis went on to destroy his first enemy aircraft on 11 October 1918, exactly a month before the end of the war; and on 18 July, 1919, it was announced that Major Edward Mannock had been awarded a posthumous Victoria Cross.

On the day that Mannock died, the Germans also lost one of their leading aces, although *Vizefeldwebel* Kurt Wusthoff of *Jasta* 4 – a pilot with twenty-seven victories – was more fortunate. He was shot down by René Fonck, but survived to become a prisoner-of-war. Fonck paid him a visit in hospital, where the German admitted to him that although the Frenchman's fame had spread throughout the German Flying Corps, no one had any idea of the tactics he used. 'That's hardly surprising,' Fonck told him wryly. 'When I attack someone, he doesn't usually live to talk about it.'

By the end of July 1918, the Allies had succeeded in turning defeat into victory, or at least the beginning of victory. Soon, the long misery of trench warfare would be over; the battle now would be for village after village, town after town, as the Germans were pushed remorselessly back across the ground they had gained. August would be a crucial month, and one that would witness, in the air, the heaviest losses suffered by both sides since the great battles of spring 1917.

Chapter Fourteen

The battles of August

On 8 August 1918 – a date later described by Ludendorff in his memoirs as 'the black day of the German Army' – the First French Army under General Debeney and General Rawlinson's Fourth British Army attacked on a fifteen-mile front east of Amiens. By three o'clock in the afternoon the Allied forces had made advances of up to seven miles and taken 7,000 prisoners; the offensive was supported by 430 tanks, the whole of the British Tank Corps less one brigade.

During the week preceding the offensive, the Allied air forces made numerous attacks on enemy airfields, notably those occupied by the *Schlachtstaffeln*, the German ground-attack squadrons. In the early hours of 5 August, two Camels of No 151 Squadron, flown by Captain S. Cockerell and Captain W.H. Haynes, carried out intruder patrols over Estrées and Guizancourt aerodromes; Cockerell arrived over Estrées just as an enemy aircraft was landing and dropped a bomb, which burst about fifty yards from it, and then turned and fired 200 rounds at it from close range. At that moment all the lights went out and Cockerell was unable to see any result, so he dropped two more bombs in the hope of hitting something before returning to base. Shortly afterwards Haynes also appeared over Estrées, having found nothing worthwhile at the other airfield, and attacked one of three Gothas which he saw approaching. The Gotha took evasive action and he lost it. He dropped his bombs on a searchlight battery and then also headed for home, his guns having jammed.

A much more successful attack was carried out at dawn, when the Camels of Nos 3 and 56 Squadrons, escorted by the Bristol Fighters of No 11 Squadron and the SE 5s of No 60 Squadron, dropped 104 25 lb bombs on Epinoy. All four squadrons then strafed the airfield, firing hundreds of rounds into the hangars, billets, workshops and the officers' mess. Two hangars received direct hits from bombs and six more were set on fire in the strafing attacks, the pilots claiming the destruction of seventeen enemy aircraft on the ground. Two very large fires were started in the workshops, and reconnaissance later revealed a pall of smoke rising to 10,000 feet over the enemy base. It is interesting to note that Nos 3 and 56 Squadrons, both of which were based at Valheureux, made a very effective partnership in this kind of operation; over a quarter of a century later, the same two units, flying Hawker Tempests as part of the Second Tactical Air Force's No 122 Wing, were also to inflict severe damage on enemy airfields in Germany in the dying months of World War Two.

On the next night, two Camels of No 151 Squadron again visited Estrées and Guizancourt. The first to arrive was Major C.J.Q. Brand, who dropped two bombs on the hangars at Guizancourt and then attacked a large two-seater which was coming in to land. He attacked it again on the ground, but broke off when all the lights went out. He remained in the vicinity of the airfield for the next half hour, dropping two bombs in the path of an aircraft which was about to touch down, then strafed the hangars and searchlights. Shortly afterwards he attacked another enemy aircraft, but was himself attacked from the rear by a German scout and returned to

Above and opposite: British observation balloons in action on the Western Front. Balloons were extremely difficult and dangerous targets.

base. In the 1939–45 war, this officer – then Air Vice-Marshal Sir Quintin Brand, DSO, MC, DFC – was to command No 10 Group, RAF Fighter Command, in the Battle of Britain. The other Camel of No 151 Squadron that night was flown by Captain Cockerell, who dropped four bombs on the hangars at Guizancourt and then shot up four searchlights until they went out. Soon afterwards he attacked a Gotha, which crash-landed some distance from the airfield.

According to one German historian,

'The fighting on this new front was of the most bitter description, and the war in the air became intense when the French as well as the English had concentrated on the new battle front. Thus the tide of battle ebbed and flowed until August 8th. On this day, a misty morning, the enemy put down intense barrage fire on the Somme Front. As soon as we realised the extent of this early morning attack, squadrons from all fronts were concentrated so rapidly upon this section of the lines, that by the time the mists had risen, a sufficient aerial force had been assembled. The day that was to prove to be a critical one in the course of the whole war, proved the most successful in our airmen's history. On the evening of that day eighty-three crashed enemy machines were counted behind our lines. Our airmen had raised the level of the whole German fighting forces by their assistance and gallantry in the battle.' *(Neumann)*

Indeed, the week from 5th to 11th August saw the heaviest losses on both sides, the RAF alone claiming the destruction of 177 enemy aircraft, with a further ninety driven down out of control, for the loss of 150 of their own. Almost every RAF bomber formation that set out was heavily attacked by enemy fighters, and as the Germans retired to new positions intense ground fire took its toll of the observation squadrons. The new Fokker D VIIs were very much in evidence; on 8 August nine of them attacked an RE 8 of No 3 Squadron AFC and shot it down, killing its crew, and on the following day the DH 9s of No 49 Squadron were subjected to persistent attacks by two large formations of Fokkers as they returned from a bombing raid. One crew – Lt J.A. Keating (an American officer) and 2nd Lt E.A. Simpson – had a particularly hard time, and it was only the observer's skill that saved them. Simpson shot down a Fokker in flames at close range, followed

Above: A British balloon ascending, with parachute bags attached.

by another shortly afterwards, and during the running fight that followed he sent two more down to crash. By this time the DH 9 had been practically shot to ribbons, and he was lucky to make a forced landing on the right side of the lines.

On the opening day of the offensive, many RAF units were assigned to ground-attack work. Among them was No 43 Squadron, its Camels now carrying an increased load of four 25 lb bombs. One of its pilots, Lt Ben Lefroy, had a very lucky escape:

'I had done my work for the day, two sorties, and was reading my mail in the mess. An orderly came haring in and asked for volunteers as a pilot in 'A' Flight had gone sick. As the only person in the mess – it was me. The only machine I could get was 'R', the target practice machine, a slow and bad machine. My own Camel was being repaired, having collected some Hun bullets on my previous sortie. Soon after coming out of cloud we ran into fifteen Huns. My engine was not good, and trying to get more out of it I 'choked' it. At this time I saw Cecil King with a couple of Huns on his tail and so pulled up to give 'em a squirt and down they came on me. The universal joint was shot off the joystick, my rudder wires cut, and petrol was squirting all over the cockpit. With the throttle I kept the nose up until, at 300 feet, I went into a spin and went in. I came to four hours later, in our barrage, with a Hun by my side. I had three bullet holes in me, both knees out of joint, fractured skull and fractured wrist – and of course a P.o.W.'

On 12 August, No 43 Squadron at Fienvillers became the first RAF unit in France to receive a fighter that was at last capable of meeting the German Flying Corps' Fokker D VIIs and Siemens-Schuckert D IIIs on more than equal terms – the Sopwith Snipe. Conceived in 1917 as a replacement for the Camel, six prototypes of the Snipe had been ordered in the autumn of that year, but a number of modifications had proven necessary and it was not until the spring of 1918 that the Snipe entered production. With 230 hp available from its very reliable Bentley BR2 rotary engine the Snipe was a potent weapon for its day, although like the Camel it was by no means easy to handle. Standard armament comprised two synchronized Vickers guns mounted in front of the cockpit. With a top speed of over 120 mph, an operational ceiling of more than 19,500 feet and an endurance of three hours, it showed a marked improvement in performance over the Camel. Visibility from the cockpit was better, too, a vital asset from the pilot's point of view. Number 43 Squadron was eventually to receive twenty-four aircraft, but it would be the middle of September before the last one was delivered and so, as the new aircraft were initially permitted to fly only defensive patrols on the British side of the lines, the Camels continued to bear the brunt of offensive operations.

On 8 August, the first day of the Allied offensive, the RAF lost forty-five aircraft in

Above: Sopwith Snipe of No 43 Sqn RAF.

Below: Sopwith Snipes of No 70 Sqn RAF.

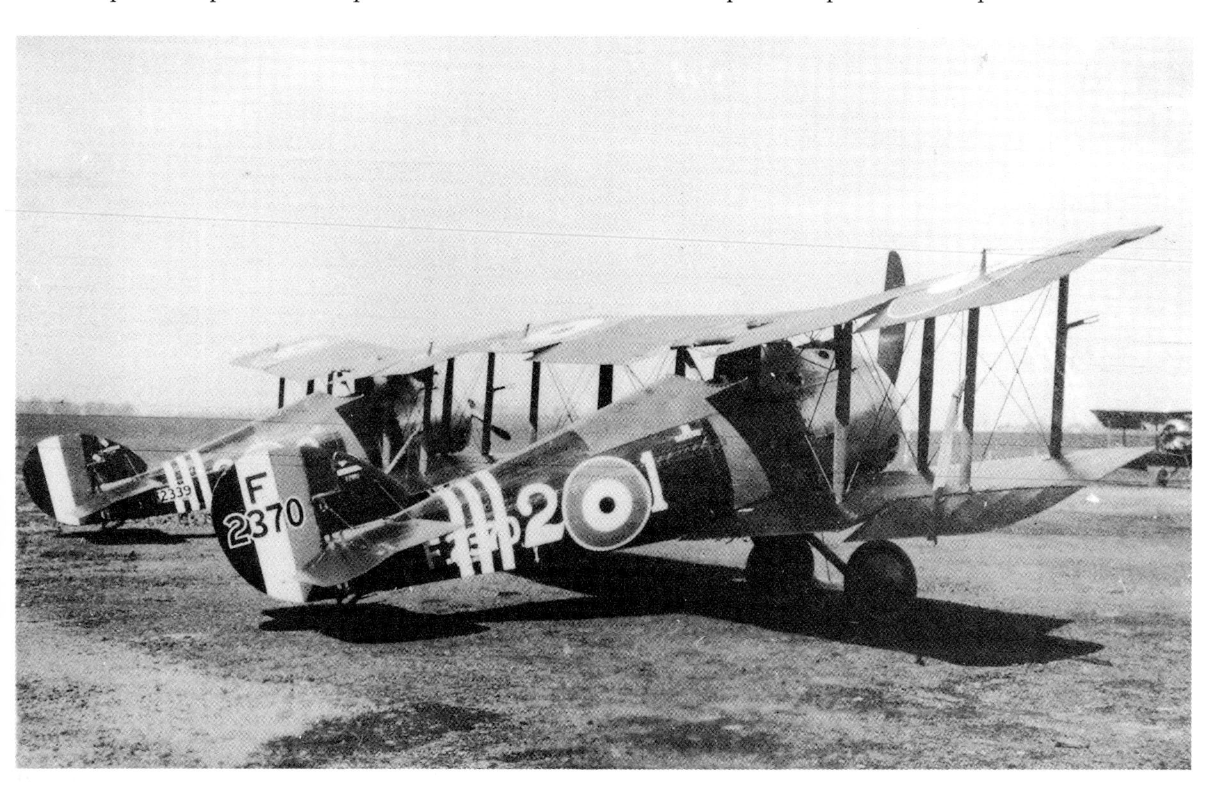

combat, with a further fifty-two wrecked on landing, a wastage rate of more than thirteen per cent. Casualties among the low flying squadrons were particularly severe, reaching twenty-three per cent. Many of the losses were sustained in attacks on bridges over the Somme, across which the Germans were retreating in considerable confusion; the tragedy was that not one of the bridges was hit. It was not until the afternoon of 9 August that a hit was at last registered on the bridge at Brie, by a DH 4 of No 205 Squadron.

There were some extraordinary adventures during those first two days of the battle. Lt Rollasson of No 209 Squadron, for example, dropped bombs from 100 feet on parties of enemy troops, but his Camel was so badly damaged by ground fire that he had to make a forced landing a few yards from some British cavalry outposts. He joined the troops, borrowed a rifle and continued to engage the enemy until someone found a horse for him, on which he returned to his aerodrome. Another pilot, Lt McKay of No 201 Squadron, wisely decided that discretion was the better part of valour; shot down by four Fokker D VIIs three hundred yards behind the enemy lines, he saw an advancing British tank and made a dash for it, but when he learned that it was about to go into action he jumped off again and zig-zagged through streams of heavy machine-gun fire to reach the British lines, out of breath but otherwise unharmed.

On 11 August, Lt C.V. Gardner of No 19 Squadron attacked one of four Pfalz Scouts, which burst into flames. Gardner saw the German pilot jump from his cockpit and deploy a parachute, the first time this had been seen in an escape from an aircraft. It is not known whether the enemy pilot landed safely. The first recorded instance of a pilot escaping by parachute from an aircraft, and surviving, occurred on 22 August 1918, when Lt Frigyes Hefty of the 42nd Scout Squadron, Austro-Hungarian Air Corps, jumped from his burning Albatros D III after a fight with Italian Hanriots over the Piave river; he made a heavy landing, but suffered no serious injury.

In another incident on 11 August, the pilot of a Pfalz Scout got a nasty shock when he attacked a No 205 Sqn DH 4 crewed by Lt W. Grossart and 2nd Lt J.S. Leach, engaged on a medium-level bombing raid. As the Pfalz completed its firing run and passed underneath the British aircraft, Leach dropped a 112 lb bomb on it. The missile smashed the Pfalz's wings and exploded on the ground.

The German Flying Corps suffered appalling losses during those crucial days of August 1918. Among the pilots killed was Erich Lowenhardt, commanding *Jasta* 10 of JG.1, who by the beginning of August had thirty-three victories, making him the third-ranking ace after von Richthofen and Udet. He was shot down on the morning of 10 August by Captain Henry Burden of No 56 Squadron during a fight between that unit's SE 5s and JG.1's D VIIs. Burden shot down two more enemy aircraft that morning, and two more later in the day. RAF pilots reported that the élite German fighter units appeared to have thrown caution to the winds in their attempts to establish air superiority over the battlefront; this was later confirmed by the biographer of Hermann Göring, who wrote that 'with a real contempt for death, the *Geschwader* suffered terrible losses owing to its reckless behaviour'.

By 11 August the Allied offensive had begun to falter as German resistance stiffened, but it had already cost the enemy 22,000 prisoners and 400 artillery pieces. In the air fighting, the recently-blooded United States Army Air Service combat squadrons were increasingly active, and their leading fighter pilots were fast emerging. Foremost among them was Lt Eddie Rickenbacker, who had several victories to his credit by the time the First Pursuit Group rearmed with SPADs in August. One of the most creditable achievements by an American pilot during the month, however, was on the first day,

Above: Rare photograph showing Sopwith Snipes, unit unidentified, in South Russia during the Allied Intervention, 1919.

when Lt Donald Hudson of the 27th Aero Squadron destroyed three enemy aircraft. His combat report tells the story.

'We were attacked by eight Fokker biplane *chasse* (fighter) machines east of Fère-en-Tardenois at 8.10 am. I tried to bank to the left and fell into a spin, and when I came out there were four enemy aircraft on my tail. I tried to turn again but fell into another spin. I was followed by the four EA down to 1,000 m. As I was coming out of the spin a machine was headed straight at me. I fired and he turned to the left; I turned a little to the left and turned back again being right on his tail. I fired about 20 rounds into him. He fell off slowly on his right wing and went into a spin. I turned on the other machines and went into a spin. When I came out the other machines were climbing up. Just as the fight began I saw an enemy plane fall off on his right wing and spin in exactly the same manner as the machine I had shot down. I saw something else fall in flames. A SPAD passed within 20 feet of my right wing, falling on its back. My engine was boiling and I could not climb as my Nourrice [coolant] was empty and by using the hand pump I just about kept going. The north-east of the railroad between Fère-en-Tardenois and Spaoney, I encountered a Rumpler biplane at between 100 and 200 m. He passed me on the right and banked up to give his observer a good shot at me. I turned and got on his tail and followed him in a circle firing right into his cockpit. Suddenly his right wing came off and he crashed. I was being fired at by machine-guns on the ground and was essing [weaving] when I noticed another Rumpler under me to my left. I turned down and fired at the observer. He disappeared and the machine crashed just inside the railroad embankment. I circled the machine once to see if either the pilot or observer got out, but they did not.'

One young American who had his first taste of air combat in August was Lt Frank Luke, a boy from Arizona who, in a brief seventeen-day

Above: Lt Frank Luke, Jr; the 'boy from Arizona'.

period of action, was to destroy eighteen enemy aircraft and balloons. Yet his first combat, on 16 August, was not particularly auspicious. His report reads:

'Saw Hun formation and followed, getting above, into the sun. The formation was strung out leaving one machine way in the rear. Being way above the formation, I cut my motor and dove down on the rear man, keeping the sun directly behind. Opened fire at about a hundred feet, keeping both guns on him until to within a few feet, then zoomed away. When I next saw him he was on his back, but looked as though he was going to come out of it, so I dove again, holding both guns on him. Instead of coming out of it he side-slipped off the opposite side, much like a falling leaf, and went down on his back.

'My last dive carried me out of reach of another machine that had turned about. They gave gave chase for about five minutes, then turned back, for I was leading (i.e. gaining on) them. My last look at the plane shot down convinced me that he struck the ground, for he was still on his back about 1,500 metres below.

'On coming home above our lines saw four EA. Started to get into the sun and above, but they saw me and dove towards me. I peaked for home. Three turned back and the other came on. I kept out of range by peaking slightly and he followed me to Coincy, where he saw one of the 95th [Squadron] boys and turned about. The 95th man could have brought down this EA if he had realized quick enough that it was an EA . . . '

Luke tried to claim the aircraft he had fired on, but it was disallowed because it had fallen in enemy territory, near Soissons, and there had been no one else to confirm it. His repeated insistence that he had shot it down did not impress his squadron colleagues, most of whom found him too cocksure and arrogant for their liking. His squadron commander shared their opinion, referring to Luke on one occasion as 'the damndest nuisance that ever stepped on to a flying field.'

Luke, in fact, came from a tough background. As a youth he had ranged the Arizona mountains on foot, carrying a seventy-pound pack, and had worked in the rough, blow-for-blow world of a copper mine. With rifle and revolver he was unsurpassed, and with his inbred spirit of adventure it was not surprising that he had been among the first to volunteer for military service when America entered the war in 1917. In September that year he enlisted in the Signal Corps and applied for assignment to the flying branch; he was quickly accepted and ordered to the School of Military Aeronautics at Austin, Texas, to undergo flying training. He proved an exceptional pilot from the beginning, completing the normal nine-week course in seven weeks, and on 23 January 1918 he was commissioned as a Second Lieutenant in the Aviation Section, Signal Officers' Reserve Corps. Six weeks later, he left for France on active service.

While the Americans helped to turn the tide of the air war overwhelmingly in the Allies' favour, those who had been in action for a long time took advantage of the August battles to add to their scores. In the *Cigognes*, René Fonck remained the master of his trade, destroying his fifty-seventh aircraft on 1 August. With the start of the Allied offensive the French pilots were mostly engaged in ground attack work and there were few air combats in their sector, although Georges Madon shot down a Fokker D VII flown by *Leutnant* Max Festler on 11 August and several more enemy aircraft were destroyed by other pilots.

On 14 August, Charles Nungesser, breaking his Parisian leave against doctor's orders, suddenly arrived at the *Cigognes'* airfield with the announcement that he had no intention of missing all the fun. That same day, he shot down four German *Drachen* observation balloons, being slightly wounded on his last sortie. But René Fonck, not to be outdone, shot down three enemy aircraft that day in the space of ten seconds; all three fell burning in a field near the village of Roye, separated by less than a hundred yards. The pilots were later identified as *Leutnant* Friedrich, *Oberfeldwebel* Arnold and *Gefreiter* Horber.

The next day, 15 August, Charles Nungesser scored his forty-fifth victory. Accompanied by *Adjudant* Henriot and *Sergent* Millot, he attacked a Fokker D VII flown by *Vizefeldwebel* Fritz Scheide and sent it down in flames. That night, in the *Cigognes'* mess, Nungesser admitted that he was feeling ill and returned to Paris, vowing to come back and increase his score to fifty. He did, in fact, return to his unit on 30 August, but he never flew in combat again.

Allied airfield attacks by day continued to be attended by success, as two extracts from the official RAF summary reveal.

August 13th. A raid was carried out by the 17th American Squadron on Varssenaere Aerodrome, in conjunction with squadrons of the 5th Group. After the first two squadrons had dropped their bombs from a low height, machines of the 17th American Squadron dived to within 200 feet of the ground and released their bombs, then proceeded to shoot at hangars and huts on the aerodrome, and a château on the NE corner of the aerodrome was also attacked with machine gun fire. The following damage was observed to be caused by this combined operation: a dump of petrol and oil was set on fire, which appeared to set fire to an ammunition dump; six Fokker biplanes were set on fire on the ground, and two destroyed by direct hits from bombs; one large Gotha hangar was set on fire and another one half demolished; a living hut was set on fire and several hangars were seen to be smouldering as a result of phosphorus bombs having fallen on them. In spite of most of the machines taking part being hit at one time or another, all returned safely, favourable ground targets being attacked on the way home. No 211 Squadron (DH 4s) bombed the aerodrome after the low flying attack was over, and demolished the château previously referred to.

August 16th. A raid was carried out on Haubourdin Aerodrome by Nos 88 and 92 Squadrons RAF and Nos 2 and 4 Squadrons AFC. Sixty-five machines took part in all, dropping 136 25 lb and six 40 lb bombs and firing a large number of rounds from a height varying from 400 to 50 feet. Three large hangars containing machines were completely burnt, and two machines standing outside were set on fire. Several fires were also started in huts, and what is believed to be the officers' mess was blown up and burnt. Several other hangars, in addition to those burnt, received direct hits. The station at Haubourdin was also attacked with machine-gun fire from a low height, causing confusion among the troops. Two staff cars were fired at, one of which upset in a ditch and another ran up a steep bank; the occupants were not observed to leave. A train was also shot at, which stopped. Considerable casualties were caused among the personnel at the aerodrome, who were seen rushing to take refuge in a hospital. All our machines returned.

On this day, No 3 Squadron AFC photographed the whole of the Australian Corps' front, while No 25 Squadron RAF (DH 4s) flew similar sorties in the adjoining sector. Almost the whole of this operation was carried out up to twenty miles behind the enemy lines and the observation aircraft were subjected to heavy attacks, but all returned safely. During this period No 8 Squadron RAF, commanded by Major Trafford Leigh-Mallory – who was later to command No 12 Group Fighter Command in the Battle of Britain – made many experiments with wireless telephony, the main object of which was to enable the crew of an observation aircraft to direct a tank's crew, but nothing practical came of it.

The reason for all the reconnaissance activity became apparent when, on 22 August, the Allies renewed their offensive on the Somme. The first British attack, on a six-mile front between the Somme and the Ancre, was thwarted by a strong German counter-attack, but the next day the main attack in the battle for Bapaume began with an advance by the British Third and Fourth Armies, supported by about 100 tanks. The British advanced some two miles, and on the 24th took the much-contested Thiepval Ridge and reached the outskirts of Bapaume. The principal objective was to take the high ground, and in this the British were successful. By 26 August their attack was spreading northwards along both banks of the River Scarpe, and twenty-four hours later the Anglo-French-American forces were advancing along the whole front. By the end of the month the Somme line had been decisively turned, twenty-three British divisions beating thirty-five German, taking 34,000 prisoners and capturing 270 guns.

Air operations during the last week of August were hampered by low clouds and rain, which helped to keep the Fokkers away from the observation aircraft, but the Germans were active during the breaks in the weather. Again, the record of No 3 Squadron AFC is fairly typical; at dawn on 23 August the RE 8s were out in support of the 1st Australian Division, which was attacking strong German natural defences in the hilly, wooded positions around Chuignes, and by the morning of the 25th the aircrews reported that the Germans were withdrawing north of the Somme. Three RE 8s, making a reconnaissance of the area near Péronne, came back with the news that it was deserted except for a few rearguards. During this phase of the battle No 3 Squadron shot down four enemy aircraft for the loss of one of its own, which crash-landed near Vauvillers.

The Germans withdrew to strong positions on the Somme bend at Péronne, the high ground near Bouchavesnes and St Quentin, and dug in. To keep the enemy on the run, the 2nd Australian Division crossed the Somme on 30 August, reaching Clery, and prepared to launch an attack on the following morning. Bad weather now forced the observation pilots to fly very low and all had narrow escapes, but only one RE 8 was lost. Attacked by thirteen enemy scouts, it was hit in the engine and had to make a forced landing in the Australian lines.

One of the most gallant fights during this period occurred on 29 August, when Lt J.M. Brown and 2nd Lt H. Lawrence, returning from a bombing raid in their No 98 Squadron DH 9, fell behind the rest of the formation through engine trouble and were attacked by twenty Fokker D VIIs. Almost at once their elevator controls were shot away, but Brown managed to retain control and dived towards the west, under constant attack. Lawrence, although badly wounded, continued fighting and shot down a Fokker in flames, sending another down out of control soon afterwards. By this time all the DH 9's petrol tanks were shot through, the engine hit in several places, and most of the instruments smashed. Lawrence, taking the brunt of the enemy fire in the rear cockpit, now had ten bullets in him; despite severe pain and loss of blood he tried to keep on firing, but his guns jammed. Brown managed to evade the attacking aircraft by diving through a cloud and crash-landed near Mory. He later received the DFC, but there is no record of Lawrence receiving any award, nor indeed of what became of him; the inference is that he died of his very severe wounds.

Among the RAF's aces who added to their scores in the August battles was Raymond Collishaw of No 203 Squadron, who shot down three more enemy aircraft; he now had fifty-eight kills to his credit. Captain Beauchamp-Proctor of No 84 Squadron concentrated on balloon attacks during the month, but managed to shoot down a two-seater on the 16th, followed by four more enemy aircraft later in the month; he was now the third surviving RAF ace after Bishop and Collishaw, a South African following two Canadians. Next in line came another Canadian, Captain D.M. MacLaren of No 46 Squadron. The Irish ace, Captain G.E.H. McElroy, now had 47 kills, and was awarded the DFC during the month to add to his MC and Bar, but he was killed in action shortly afterwards.

On 27 August, a Sopwith Camel pilot of No 209 Squadron was attacked by a Halberstadt; he promptly turned on it and fired 250 rounds into it, killing its observer, and the German aircraft spun down to crash. A few minutes later the same pilot attacked a Hannoveraner; its wings crumpled up and it went down to crash in a wood.

It was the Camel pilot's seventh victory. 'Wop' May had learned a lot since his career had very nearly been terminated by Manfred von Richthofen five months earlier.

Chapter Fifteen
Bloody September

The third phase of the great British offensive on the Somme began on 2 September 1918, when the Canadian Corps of General Horne's First Army and the 17th Corps of General Byng's Third Army breached the enemy defences on a six-mile front between Drocourt and Queant. On the following day, English, Scottish and Naval troops under General Fergusson broke through the Queant-Pronville defences. In those two days, the British forces took 34,000 German prisoners. The offensive unfolded in heavy rain and no real degree of air support was available until 8.00 am on the first day, but after that the army co-operation squadrons operated full out, bombing and strafing the retreating enemy as well as bringing back valuable information on his movements. Much depended on the success of the Canadian advance, which was followed throughout by two RE 8s of No 13 Squadron; their reports enabled the commander of the 57th and 63rd Naval Divisions, on the flank of the Canadians, to commit his troops to action at exactly the right time.

In parallel with the British assault, General Mangin's French forces advanced to the north of Soissons. The *Cigognes*, as usual, were in the thick of the fighting; on 3 September Georges Madon gained his fortieth victory, a two-seater flown by *Vizefeldwebel* Max Sievert. By this time, most of the leading fighter units of the German Flying Corps had been concentrated in the Somme sector to meet the threat of the British advance, and the kills scored by the French pilots were mostly against observation aircraft or *Drachen* balloons.

The United States Army Air Service continued to operate alongside the French. Early in September, Captain Eddie Rickenbacker was appointed to command the 94th Squadron; it was a bold decision on the part of his superiors, because other flight commanders were senior to to him. Nevertheless, his all-round experience matched that of the others, and in some respects, such as technical skill, he excelled. He was also a very fine leader, a man who took the utmost care of the pilots he led into action. At this time, Rickenbacker had six victories to his credit.

His superiors' faith in him was soon justified. He assumed command of the 94th at a time when there was keen rivalry between it and its sister unit, the 27th Aero Squadron, and at the beginning of September the 27th had managed to creep ahead in the tally of enemy aircraft destroyed. This was a major source of annoyance to Rickenbacker, partly because the 27th was a newer unit than his own, and his first act on taking command was to assemble all the squadron personnel and deliver a strong pep talk. To the mechanics, he pointed out that the 27th's machines were seldom on the ground because of technical trouble, and that he expected to see a rapid rise in maintenance standards. From the pilots, he expected a comparable rise in the standard of tactics and teamwork; when they were not fighting they would train arduously until that standard had been reached.

These were tough words from a new commander, and had they been delivered by anyone other than Rickenbacker they might have caused bitter resentment. As it was, he achieved his object, and from that day the 94th set out to be better than any other unit. To prove his point, Rickenbacker set out on a lone patrol on 15 September. Over the lines he sighted two LVG two-seaters with an escort of five Fokker D VIIs above and behind. Climbing into the sun, he dived on the Fokkers and shot one of them down. The others scattered, and Rickenbacker continued his dive on the two-seaters. Running the gauntlet of fire from both enemy observers, he engaged the first LVG and then pulled up in a stall turn to repeat the attack. He carried out this manoeuvre several times, firing at each LVG in turn, and eventually got into a position to make a beam attack on the first LVG, keeping it between himself and the second enemy aircraft. He gave it a long burst and it went down in flames. Rickenbacker then broke off the attack and headed for home, with the Fokkers still milling around in confusion overhead, having gained his eighth and ninth victories.

Three days earlier, on 12 September, the Americans had lost one of their leading aces. Lieutenant David Putnam, like so many other Americans, had found his way into the *Aviation Militaire* by way of the French Foreign Legion, and had flown successively with SPA 94, 156 and 38. As a corporal, he destroyed his first enemy aircraft on 19 January 1918, and by July his score had risen to eleven confirmed. He was then commissioned into the USAAS and assigned to the 139th Aero Squadron, with which unit he destroyed two more enemy aircraft on 15 and 22 August. On 12 September, during a patrol with Lt Robertson in the St Mihiel area, he encountered six Fokker D VIIs and, in the ensuing battle, was shot down and killed. His aircraft crashed at Limey and he was buried with full military honours at Toul.

In support of the French land offensive, the *Aviation Militaire* stepped up its daylight bombing attacks on targets in western Germany, and they too encountered the formidable Siemens-Schuckert D III. *Vizefeldwebel* Fritz Beckhardt, a pilot with *Kampfeinsitzerstaffel* 5 (No 5 Single-Seat Fighter Squadron) described one encounter:

> 'At around 7.00 am we were suddenly alerted to deal with several enemy formations which had been reported approaching from the direction of Haguenau. We clambered into the cockpits of our D.IIIs and took off from Lahr-Dinglingen airfield. We were not flying in formation, and our aircraft were scattered over a wide area. Suddenly, high above me, I saw two tiny specks. Aircraft flying on a north-easterly course at an altitude of 20,000–23,000 feet. I pulled back the nose of my D III, opened the throttle fully and climbed after the intruders at full power. Owing to the superlative climbing performance of my aircraft, I was soon approaching the altitude of the enemy bombers, which I identified as Breguet 14s.
>
> When I reached an altitude only some 900 feet below the French aircraft, I loosed a couple of bursts from my machine-guns in an attempt to divert them from their target. One of the Breguets lost height rapidly. I put the nose of my D.III down a little in order to gain speed, caught up with the Frenchman and turned in to attack. Suddenly, a burst of machine-gun fire came from behind, and I hastily flung my D.III round in a climbing turn to find that the other Breguet had followed me down and had got on my tail. Out of the corner of my eye I noticed with satisfaction that the pilot of the crippled Breguet had apparently lost his sense of direction and was heading away from his own lines. A burst from my Spandaus put the gunner of the second Breguet out of action. I overshot the bomber, turned, and came up under my opponent, firing a long burst into the Breguet's belly. The Frenchman immediately went into a spin. I now turned my attention to the first machine which was still trying vainly to escape, but he proved easy meat, crashing into the river north of Kehl.'

In September, an improved model of the Siemens-Schuckert design also began to reach the German fighter squadrons. It had a completely redesigned upper wing and was designated SSW D IV. The maximum speed, at 118 mph, was only slightly better than the D III's, but the rate of climb was much better, the D IV being able to reach 19,700 feet in sixteen or seventeen minutes. The first deliveries of the D IV were made to *Jasta* 14 and *Kampfeinsitzerstaffel* 2 at Saarbrucken, *Jasta* 22 and JG.2 'Boelcke'. A few were assigned to home defence duties to the *Marine-Jagdeschwader*, the German Navy's air defence wing. *Leutnant* Alfred Lenz, commanding *Jasta* 22, reported that

> 'The SSW D.IV is undoubtedly far superior to any single-seat fighter at the front today. This superiority manifests itself pimarily in the climb rate and manoeuvrability of the fighter, and in maximum level speeds at altitudes above 13,000 feet.
>
> On 29 September, whilst on a sortie, I reached an altitude of 19,685 feet in 14.5 minutes. The time was carefully recorded by the cockpit chronometer and altimeter which were thoroughly checked for accuracy after completion of the sortie. During this sortie a British photo-reconnaissance aircraft and its escorting S.E.5 were outclimbed with the greatest of ease, and the S.E.5 was shot down during a climbing turn.'

Fortunately for the Allies, the SSW D IV came too late. Large orders were placed, but only 280 fighters of this type were delivered before the end of hostilities.

On 2 September, there occurred a curious incident in which a body of German troops surrendered to a British aircraft. Lieutenants A. Ibbotson and W.J. Carruthers, flying an RE 8 of No 59 Squadron on the lookout for an enemy counter-attack, sighted sixty-five Germans sheltering in a trench and a sunken road. The Germans fired at them, whereupon Ibbotson dived and fired back, killing one and wounding three. As he turned to make a second attack, he saw that the enemy troops were waving a white flag. Throttling back, he descended to fifty feet and flew slowly past, he and Carruthers

Below and the following three photographs: The Siemens-Schuckert SSW D IV was a formidable fighter, but it came into service too late to influence the course of the air war.

indicating by hand signals that the Germans were to head towards the British lines with their hands up. The enemy troops complied, and the RE 8 circled overhead until its crew were certain that they had been taken prisoner.

The attitude displayed by these German soldiers was becoming increasingly typical; they were losing the will to fight. Also, the apparent absence of the German Flying Corps led to much criticism. A German historian recorded that

> 'The irritation of the infantry found its expression in such remarks as: 'May God punish England, our artillery, and our Air Force ' or, a question passed from man to man as loudly as they dared: 'Has anybody here seen a German airman?' As a result of this frame of mind, numerous orders were issued by the Army Corps, which further displeased the Air Force and led to undisciplined and unofficial replies . . . Our scanty defensive resources were being used almost all night and day, for fear of attacks from the air, although they effected nothing beyond using up petrol, wearing out engines, and so occupying personnel as to prevent them from doing more serious work.
>
> 'The monthly production of aeroplanes was not even sufficient to provide each squadron with the same type throughout. Thus, for example, (Observation) Squadron 23 was composed of five different types.'

At the beginning of the September battle the German pilots generally showed a lack of aggression, only occasionally showing flashes of their old determination. On 5 September, the SE 5s of No 92 Squadron fought a hectic battle with a strong formation of Fokker D VIIs; the squadron commander, Major A. Coningham (later Air Vice-Marshal Arthur Coningham, commander of the Desert Air Force in 1941–2) attacked the German leader's aircraft, which went into a steep climb and then turned over on its back. Coningham saw the German pilot fall out, cling desperately to the edge of the cockpit for a few seconds as the aircraft went into a spin, then lose his grip and plunge to earth near Cambrai.

Another 92 Squadron pilot, Lt E. Shapard, had just shot down a D VII when he was attacked from behind by several more. Boxed in, he put his aircraft into a spin in an effort to escape, recovering almost at ground level and returning to base with his wheels almost touching the ground. He had been lucky: the main spars of all four mainplanes had been shot through, his fuselage longerons had been smashed and there was a bullet in one of his magnetos.

The next day, the Bristol Fighter once again proved its worth when a flight of No 20 Squadron aircraft was attacked by Fokker D VIIs. One of the enemy aircraft passed directly in front of the Bristol flown by Captain H.P. Lale, who shot it down in flames, and at the same time a second Fokker was destroyed by his observer, 2nd Lt H.L. Edwards. Meanwhile, Lt A.C. Iaccaci – one of the Americans in the RAF – manoeuvred his Bristol so that his observer, Lt A. Mills, could get in a series of effective bursts at more attackers. One broke up in mid-air and another went down to crash, exploding in flames on impact. A fifth D VII was shot down by Sgt A. Newland, the observer in another Bristol.

From 9 to 14 September flying was severely curtailed over the northern sectors of the front by gale force winds and heavy rainstorms, but after that the tempo quickly picked up again, and the last two weeks of the month saw heavy fighting. In the early hours of 16 September, Lt F.C. Broome of No 151 Squadron achieved a notable success by shooting down a five-engined Giant bomber; after firing 500 rounds at it, he saw it burst into flames and fall on the British side of the lines. Two nights earlier, during one of the few spells when the wind dropped, Captain W.H. Haynes and Lt E.P. Mackay, also of No 151 Squadron, had destroyed a Gotha apiece. The RAF's night fighters were beginning to cost the enemy dearly.

During one of the early patrols of 16 September, Lt W.T. Martin and Sgt M. Jones, flying a Bristol Fighter of No 22 Squadron, attacked a formation of Fokker D VIIs, one of which they shot down. They were then attacked in turn and had their aileron wires shot away; the Bristol side-slipped, almost out of control, through 2,000 feet. Sergeant Jones, realizing the peril of the situation, climbed out on to the bottom wing and stood there, clinging to a strut, until his weight righted the aircraft. Martin was able to land the aircraft in friendly territory, and Jones was later awarded the DFM.

Another Bristol Fighter crew, Captain E.S. Coler and 2nd Lt E.J. Corbett of No 11 Squadron, also had a lucky escape that day. While out on a reconnaissance they were attacked by a large number of Fokker D VIIs, which shot away their aileron controls and put a bullet through one of their petrol tanks. Coler dived to 1,000 feet over Cambrai, still under attack, and two of the Fokkers overshot. Coler got behind one and shot it down; the other, which had turned quickly away and was not coming in for a stern attack, was shot down by Corbett. The Bristol Fighter staggered back across the lines at 150 feet and Coler, realizing that it was rapidly going out of control, used a combination of rudder, elevator and throttle to nurse it towards the ground in a slow sideslip. One set of wings struck first and absorbed most of the impact, the crew climbing from the wreck relatively unharmed.

It must have seemed to the Bristol Fighter crews, in the last fortnight of September, that they were bearing the brunt of the enemy's rediscovered aggression. On the 17th, Lts Frank Jeffreys and F.W. Addison, out on reconnaissance in an aircraft of No 88 Squadron, were attacked by six Fokker D VIIs. Addison shot down the first one, and another, which for a few terrifying moments seemed bent on ramming the Bristol, suddenly fell away on its back with its starboard wing in tatters. The remaining Fokkers harried the Bristol until it crossed the lines, one bullet grazing Addison's hand and putting his gun out of action. The aircraft landed with both its petrol tanks shot through.

On 20 September, Bristol Fighters of No 20 Squadron, together with SE 5s of No 84 Squadron, fought a half-hour battle with twenty Fokker D VIIs over St Quentin. Throughout the battle the RAF aircraft were at a great disadvantage because of a very strong westerly wind, which drove them progressively deeper into enemy territory. The Bristols quickly got the measure of their opponents; Lt F.G. Harlock dived on one and shot it down, while his observer, 2nd Lt A.S. Draisey, disposed of another. A third Fokker was shot down by Lt F.E. Boulton and Sgt Mitchell, and a fourth by Lt M. McCall and 2nd Lt C. Boothroyd. While the fight was in progress, another Bristol, flown by Captain T.P. Middleton with Lt A. Mills as his observer, arrived and joined in; they engaged four Fokkers, two of which they shot down.

The battle was then joined by the SE 5s of No 84 Squadron led by Captain C.F. Falkenberg, who announced his arrival by shooting down one Fokker and driving another off the tail of a Bristol Fighter. Six more Fokkers were engaged by 2nd Lt W.J.B. Nel, also of No 84 Sqn, who destroyed one and then escorted a damaged Bristol towards the lines. On the way home the pair were attacked by seven Fokkers and Nel was obliged to take refuge in a cloud; the Bristol Fighter never returned.

On 16 September, the *Cigognes* suffered a grievous loss. Lieutenant Maurice Boyau had made a name for himself as an international rugby player before the war, having been capped for France eleven times and captained the side; like so many others of his type he was attracted to aviation, and by October 1917 he had ten victories to his credit – six balloons and four aircraft. (Unlike the British, the French counted observation balloons in a pilot's total list of kills – a justifiable procedure, since attacking them was an extremely dangerous venture.)

Between 28 May and 4 June 1918 Boyau shot down five aircraft and two balloons, and by mid-July his score stood at twenty-nine. On 11 August he destroyed a balloon and a two-seater, then went off on leave, returning to the front on 13 September. In the next two days he shot down four more balloons; then, at 10.00 am on 16 September, he set out on an offensive patrol with a corporal named Walla. General Mangin's forces were fighting for the Chemin des Dames, and had requested the *Cigognes* to knock down some troublesome *Drachens*.

Neither pilot returned. Then, two days later, the news came in that Corporal Walla was lying gravely wounded in a French military hospital with an incendiary bullet in his back. He was able to give a few details of what had happened.

It seemed that Boyau had made three attacks on a balloon about six miles inside the enemy lines, sending it down in flames on his third pass. At that moment he and Walla were attacked by seven Fokker D VIIs. Walla, obeying Boyau's earlier instructions, turned away and sped for the French lines, running the gauntlet of heavy machine-gun fire from the ground and pursued by the Fokkers. Boyau also turned, passing directly under the falling balloon, then pulled his SPAD round to engage the Fokkers while Walla made good his escape. Looking back, Walla saw Boyau's aircraft hit by ground fire; it burst into flames at once and went down to crash. Walla, wounded by a burst of fire from one of the Fokkers, managed to make a crash-landing in friendly territory.

The next day, the pilots of Boyau's unit, *Escadrille* SPA 77, arranged a rugby match. They played with fourteen men, and fourteen appeared on the photograph that was taken afterwards. Boyau's position was wing forward, and it was left vacant; but his name was recorded beneath it.

René Fonck, as usual, was on top form. On 26 September he destroyed six enemy aircraft in one day, the second time he had accomplished this feat. In the morning, flying from Chalons-sur-Marne, he destroyed two Fokker D VIIs and a two-seater; two more Fokkers and an Albatros fell to his guns in the afternoon. The Albatros broke up in mid-air and the pilot, tumbling from the cockpit, narrowly missed hitting Fonck's SPAD. Fonck landed back at base trembling and soaked in sweat; the strain, at last, was beginning to tell. At this point, he had scored sixty-six victories.

By 24 September, the Allies were pushing against the last and greatest of the enemy's defences, the Hindenburg Line, which consisted of a vast network of concrete pillboxes, carefully sited trenches and barbed wire. Foch's plan was to attack it in four places, and allotted the sector running fromSt Quentin to Cambrai to the British. They faced a formidable task, for the St Quentin Canal had been incorporated as part of the defensive line and for a stretch of 6,000 yards it ran underground, providing excellent cover close to the front line for several thousand troops.

The assault was to be made by the First, Third and Fourth British Armies, supported by over 1,000 aircraft in twenty-seven fighter, four fighter-reconnaissance, seven day bomber, six night bomber and thirteen Corps squadrons. For several days prior to the offensive, the German bombers made determined efforts to attack British supply dumps and other targets in the rear areas, and suffered heavily at the hands of No 151 Squadron's Camels. On 21 September Lt F.C. Broome chased a Gotha in bright moonlight and opened fire from 200 yards. It fell in flames and disintegrated in the explosion of its own bombs. On the following night, Major Quintin Brand made a close-range attack on another Gotha, which went into a steep climb before falling over on its back and going into an inverted spin. Brand lost it, but British troops later confirmed that it had crashed near Gouzeaucourt. During the same patrol, Brand and another 151 Squadron pilot, Lt J.H. Summers, attacked and destroyed a large enemy two-seater near Bourlon, and the squadron's hat-trick that night was completed by Lt A.A. Mitchell, who drove down a Gotha and saw it crash while attempting to land in a field.

On 24 September, when rain and low cloud gave way to a spell of fine weather, there was some intense air fighting as the RAF fighter squadrons battled to keep the enemy away from the reconnaissance aircraft that were engaged in photographing the Hindenburg Line defences. Other squadrons carried out bombing and strafing attacks on targets of opportunity behind the enemy lines, and it was during one of these that Captain E.J. McLaughty of No 4 Squadron AFC nearly came to grief. He had just dropped a pair of 25 lb bombs on the rear end of a train, derailing it, when he was attacked by an enemy two-seater, which he shot down. He was then attacked by seven Fokker D VIIs and wounded, but kept on fighting. He got in a burst at one of the Fokkers, which broke up, but then his ammunition ran out and he had no choice but to break off combat. Two Fokkers got on his tail, but he frightened them off by firing Very flares at them. McLaughry then passed out, and regained consciousness only just in time to right his aircraft and crash-land on the British side of the lines. This action, the culmination of months of gallant work by the Australian, earned him the DSO; he returned to command No 4 Squadron in October, having recovered from his wounds and been promoted major.

The other Australian fighter squadron, No 2, had considerable success on 24 September, destroying five Fokker D VIIs in one fight. A similar success was enjoyed by No 148 (American) Squadron, which destroyed five out of seven D VIIs in a dogfight over Bourlon Wood. One of the pilots who scored in this engagement was Lt Field Kindley, who had shot down No 148's first German in July. Kindley survived the war with twelve victories, only to die in a flying accident at San Antonio, Texas, in 1920. The USAF's Kindley Air Force Base on Bermuda was named after him.

Airfield attacks were stepped up once again. On 26 September, eleven SE 5s of No 40 Squadron and fourteen Camels of No 203, escorted by Bristol Fighters of No 22 Squadron, carried out a very low level attack on Lieu St Amand aerodrome. No 40 Squadron went in first, their bombs setting fire to a large hangar; then No 203 came in, setting four hangars ablaze and obtaining direct hits on some huts. During the attack, Major Raymond Collishaw spotted a Fokker D VII taking off and shot it down; two DFWs were strafed on the ground by other pilots and left burning. On their way home, the RAF pilots encountered a number of Fokker D VIIs, two of which were shot down by a crew of No 22 Squadron and a third by Collishaw.

It was Collishaw's sixty-second and final victory. Soon afterwards, he was sent back to Canada to help form the Royal Canadian Air Force, but this was delayed by the end of the war and so Collishaw remained in the RAF with a permanent commission. In November 1918 he was given command of No 47 Squadron, which he took to South Russia as part of the Allied Intervention Force, fighting for the Tsarist Russians under General Denikin. Following the collapse of that unhappy venture, Collishaw served in various commands until, in 1939, he was appointed Air Officer Commanding Middle East Bomber Group with the rank of Air Commodore. When the Italians entered the war he took command of No 204 Group, whose motley collection of aircraft he used to good effect in carrying out hard-hitting airfield attacks which thoroughly demoralized the enemy. Just how effective his scheme had proved was revealed when British forces invaded Cyrenaica and found over 1,000 Italian aircraft immobilized on their airfields, either wrecked in air attacks or starved of spare parts. Collishaw was promoted Air Vice-Marshal and, after a spell as AOC No 14 Group at Inverness, he retired in 1943. After a successful career in business, he died in September 1976.

While the British were preparing to assault the Hindenburg Line, the Americans were on the offensive in the St Mihiel sector, and the last two weeks of September saw fierce fighting over that embattled area. Lieutenant Frank Luke was at last beginning to prove his qualities in action by destroying enemy observation balloons; he had now teamed up with another young pilot, Lt Joe Wehner, and together they made a formidable pair. On 18 September, after destroying half a dozen balloons between them during the two preceding days – always fighting their way through strong opposition – they fought a particularly hard battle, as Luke's combat report tells.

> 'Lieutenant Wehner and I left the airdrome at sixteen hours to spot enemy balloons. Over St Mihiel we saw two German balloons near Labeuville. Maneuvred in the clouds and dropped down, burning both. We were then attacked by a number of EA, the main formation attacking Lt Wehner, who was above and on one side. I started climbing to join the fight when two EA attacked me from the rear. I turned on them, opening both guns on the leader. We came head on until within a few yards of each other when my opponent turned to one side in a nose dive and I saw him crash to the ground.
>
> I then turned on the second, shot a short burst, and he turned and went into a dive. I saw a number of EA above but could not find Lt Wehner, so turned and made for our lines. The above fight occurred in the vicinity of St Hilaire. On reaching our balloon lines, flew east. Saw Archie (AA fire) on our side, flew towards it, and found an enemy observation machine. I gave chase with some other SPADs and got him off from his lines. After a short encounter he crashed within our lines, southeast of Verdun. Lieutenant Wehner is entitled to share in the victories over both the balloons. Confirmations requested, two balloons and three planes.'

As soon as he got back to base, Luke went to seek out Joe Wehner. But Wehner would not be coming back; he had gone down in flames over Labeuville.

Luke was inconsolable, for Wehner was the only real friend he had ever had. His commanding officer sent him off on a fortnight's leave to Paris, but Luke returned after only a week, thirsting to be back in action. He sought and obtained permission to move up to an old French airfield closer to the front line. His new wingman was Lt Ivan Roberts, and the pair made their first flight together on 26 September. Over Sivy they had a dogfight with five Fokkers; Luke sent one down out of control, but had to break off the fight when his guns jammed. On his return he found that Roberts was missing. The lieutenant was never seen again.

It was Joe Wehner all over again, and Luke was plunged into deeper gloom than ever. On 27 September he absented himself from his squadron, with his aircraft, and was gone until the following morning, when he returned and reported that he had paid a visit to the *Cigognes*. He also added that he had got another balloon.

His CO administered a severe reprimand, telling Luke that he was grounded until further notice. Luke went out in a rage and a few minutes later, despite his CO's order, he took off again, heading for the French airfield near Verdun. The day before, he had pinpointed the positions of three more balloons, and he was determined to get them, even though he knew that he might have to face a court martial when he returned.

Luke got his three balloons, but never had to face the court. Wounded in the shoulder by ground fire, he side-slipped down to land in a field. Climbing from the cockpit, he fought off advancing enemy troops with his revolver until they shot him dead. His last, gallant action was to earn him a posthumous Medal of Honor.

But the finest tribute to Luke's courage was paid by the man who had suffered most at his hands: *Leutnant* Mangels, the commander of the balloon company in the Verdun sector. It was Mangels' machine-gunners who had shot Luke down, and he was one of the first officers to reach the scene, in a muddy field near Murvaux. Mangels ended his report on the incident with these words.

> 'His insignia I took and kept in remembrance of this great and fearless sportsman. He was a man of dazzling courage, one of the bravest we fought in the war.'

Chapter Sixteen
Last act: October–November 1918

The British assault on the Hindenburg Line began at 5.30 am on 27 September 1918, and by nightfall it was clear that the attack was meeting with success all along the line; the Canal du Nord had been crossed in several places and the enemy had lost 10,000 prisoners, as well as 200 guns.

The part played by the RAF's army co-operation squadrons in this early victory was enormous. Before the battle, an elaborate system of air-ground co-ordination had been devised and rehearsed exhaustively between aircraft and artillery batteries, so that despite the swift movement of the battlefront the aircraft were able to direct the guns with great accuracy. Enemy aircraft were active all along the front, and the Corps squadrons took some punishment. Early on the 27th, for example, Lt R.E. Britton and 2nd Lt B. Hickman of No 13 Squadron, flying an RE 8, were attacked by eight Fokker D VIIs. Hickman was wounded early in the engagement but went on firing, sending one Fokker down out of control. A minute later Britton was wounded too, and in trying to take evasive action put the RE into a spin. He recovered just in time and landed in a field behind the German lines. As the Fokker circled overhead, the RAF men slumped in their cockpits and pretended to be dead. The ruse worked and the Fokker flew off without strafing the RE; as soon as it was safely out of sight Britton took off again and flew back to the squadron's base at Mory, but passed out just as he was about to touch down and crashed. Both occupants were pulled from the wreck alive.

One unit that was very active during the attack on the Hindenburg Line, and the period leading up to it, was No 79 Squadron, armed with Sopwith Dolphins. No 79 was one of four squadrons on the Western Front to use the Dolphin – the others being Nos 19, 23 and 87 – and, after early misgivings, the pilots were discovering that it was an excellent combat aircraft. Designed as a Camel replacement, the Dolphin was unpopular at first with its pilots; the 220 hp Hispano-Suiza engine was virtually in the pilot's lap, with his face uncomfortably close to the butts of the overhead twin Lewis guns; he had a square steel-tube cockpit frame around his neck and the fuel tank was directly behind him. However, the Dolphin was heavily armed; in addition to the Lewis guns, which were mounted on the upper wing attachment frame to fire forward and upward, twin Vickers guns were mounted under the engine decking. (In practice, the Lewis guns were found to be more of a hindrance than a help, and one or both were often removed. Some 87 Squadron Dolphins had them remounted on the lower wings, outboard of the propeller arc.) The Dolphin's top speed was 120 mph, and ceiling was 19,000 feet.

In the week before the offensive No 79 Squadron destroyed nine enemy aircraft, four being shot down by 'A' Flight commander, Captain R.B. Bannerman. Then, on the 28th, the Squadron destroyed seven hostile machines in the course of the day, most of them in one battle during the afternoon when the pilots went to the rescue of a Bristol Fighter which was being attacked by ten Fokker D.VIIs. One was shot down by Lt F.W. Gillet, who had also claimed a two-seater on an earlier patrol, two by Lt J. McNeaney, and one each by Captain Bannerman, Captain F.I. Lord and Lt F. Woolley.

The assault on the main Hindenburg Line defences, between Bellenglise and Vendhuille, was launched on Sunday 29 September. Captured German documents had provided the British commanders with details of every German defensive position, as well as supply dumps and communications centres, and these were subjected to heavy shelling and also bombing attacks as long as the weather permitted. Progress was swift – too swift in some areas, such as the sector in which the US 27th Division pushed on too far and found itself cut off in smoke and fog that made it impossible for pilots on contact patrol to see flares and other signals. As a result, the Americans suffered heavily. Bad weather on the last day of the month also made it impossible for the RAF to give full support to the ground forces, and enemy resistance was stubborn. Nevertheless, by nightfall on the 30th the British forces had taken the St Quentin Canal, almost all the Hindenburg Line defences had been overwhelmed, and German resistance was beginning to crumble. Soon, in the autumn rain and mist, on roads clogged by the Flanders mud that had been the misery of millions of men for four years, the battered but still undefeated German armies were trudging back the way they had come in 1914.

Much of the Allied air effort during this phase was devoted to attacks on road junctions, railway stations and other bottlenecks. The German Flying Corps continued to fight fiercely, if spasmodically, and to inflict losses on the Allied day bombers, although in doing so their own losses were far from light. On 1 October, for instance, DH 9s of No 108 Squadron had just attacked Ingelmunster station when they were intercepted by thirty-three enemy scouts. A running fight developed, and in the next ten minutes, during which the DH 9s managed to stay in close formation and provide good mutual defensive fire support, they shot down four of the enemy without loss.

During the first week in October the two Australian fighter squadrons, No 2 with its SE 5s and No 4 with its Camels, were very active, carrying out many ground-attack sorties against enemy airfields and lines of communication. Number 4 Squadron in particular received several mentions in the official communiques, beginning on 2 October:

> 'Lieutenants O.B. Ramsay and C.V. Ryrie, 4 Squadron AFC, left the ground at 4.45 am to attack Don Railway Station, where they dropped four 25 lb bombs, observing one direct hit; they then dropped four more bombs on Houplin aerodrome and fired at machines and mechanics on the aerodrome from 700 feet. A train steaming out of Haubourdin was also fired at and made to pull up.'

Then, on 5 October:

'A patrol of No 4 Squadron AFC, consisting of Captain R. King, 2nd Lieutenant T.H. Barkell and 2nd Lieutenant A.J. Palliser, during a flight of 1 hour 20 minutes, carried out the following work: Destroyed one balloon in flames; dropped twelve 25 lb bombs from a low height on a train in Avelin station and on the aerodrome, obtaining four direct hits on the station and one on a shed on the aerodrome. They also fired a large number of rounds into a "flaming onion" battery, and three times attacked horse transport, which scattered in confusion. The sheds on Avelin aerodrome were also shot up, and finally a train was fired at, one wagon of which exploded, completely wrecking two trucks.'

With the end of the war in sight, and enemy aircraft absent from the front for lengthy periods, the leading Allied fighter pilots flew intensively, keen on adding to their scores. By the end of October, Eddie Rickenbacker of the 94th Aero Squadron had scored twenty-six victories, putting him well ahead of any other

American pilot; the next in line was Captain W.C. Lambert of the RAF, with twenty-two, followed by Captain A.T. Iaccaci (RAF) and Frank Luke with eighteen, Captain F.W. Gillet (RAF) and Raoul Lufbery with seventeen, then Captains H.A. Kuhlberg and O.J. Rose (both RAF) with sixteen each.

As the American pilots serving in the RAF had been in action longer than their USAS counterparts, the achievements of Rickenbacker and Luke were all the more noteworthy. Rickenbacker – whose score would undoubtedly have been higher had not an ear infection debarred him from flying between the end of May and mid-September – survived the war and was awarded the Medal of Honor; he was later active in both the automobile and airline industries and was largely responsible for building up Eastern Airlines, of which he became chairman in 1953. During the Second World War he toured widely, visiting USAAF units overseas. On one flight across the Pacific his aircraft had to ditch, and he and his crew spent twenty-one days on a liferaft before being rescued. He remained active in various fields until his death in July 1973, at the age of eighty-two.

In the *Cigognes*, René Fonck scored his sixty-eighth and sixty-ninth victories on 5 October. There was no one to come near him now, but sightings of enemy aircraft were so infrequent that it would be the end of the month before he scored again.

Meanwhile, in the north, the RAF took its latest fighter, the Sopwith Snipe, into action during these final weeks. No 43 Squadron had begun offensive patrols with its new Snipes on 26 September; these mostly involved bomber escort or diversionary patrols in conjunction with bombing raids, and in six days the pilots claimed the destruction of ten enemy aircraft for no loss. Unfortunately, only two of the enemy machines could be confirmed, these being credited to Lts E. Mulcair and R.S. Johnston. Throughout October No 43 continued to fly escort missions, often with the DH 9s of Nos 98 and 107 Squadrons. On occasions the Snipe pilots would also indulge in some bombing; on 23 October, for example, they obtained several direct hits with 25 lb Cooper bombs – four of which could be carried beneath the Snipe's fuselage – on the railway station at Hirson.

In October a second unit, No 4 Squadron AFC, also began to exchange its Camels for Snipes at Serny. The first patrol with the new aircraft was flown on the 26th, when nine Snipes led by Lts T.C.R. Baker and T.H. Barkell engaged fifteen Fokker D VIIs over Tournai. Barkell, although wounded in the leg, shot down two of the enemy, while Lts Baker, E.J. Richards and H.W. Ross got one each. On the following day the squadron lost Lt F. Howard, shot down and killed in a dogfight over the same area.

The next three days saw some of the greatest air battles of the war as the German Flying Corps threw its dwindling reserves into action against the Allied aircraft that were now swarming everywhere behind the enemy lines. On 28 October, fifteen Snipes of No 4 Squadron AFC, led by Captain A.T. Cole, came upon twelve Fokker D VIIs which were attacking a formation of DH 9s over Peruwelz and destroyed five of the enemy for no loss. Later in the day, ten Snipes under Captain R. King were detailed to escort twelve SE 5as of No 2 Squadron AFC in a bombing attack on Lessines, north of Ath on the Dendre river. The SEs carried out their bombing attack and then climbed to join the Snipes, which were engaging about thirty Fokkers. By the time the SEs arrived the fight was virtually over; two of the Fokkers had been destroyed by Lt A.J. Palliser, a third by Major W.A. McLaughty and a fourth by Lt T.C.R. Baker, who had already shot down a D VII while out on patrol by himself that morning. Another Fokker was destroyed by Lt E.L. Simonson of No 2 Squadron, who shot the enemy off a Snipe's tail.

In the afternoon of 29 October, fifteen Snipes of No 4 Squadron in two flights under King and Baker were patrolling near Tournai in fine but hazy weather when they encountered an equal number of Fokker D VIIs at 14,000 feet. Conscious that there were other strong formations of Fokkers in the area – probably sixty aircraft in all – the Australians quickly engaged the first gaggle, which was apparently preparing to attack some Allied two-seaters lower down. A fierce battle ensued, during which two Fokkers were shot down in flames by Lt G. Jones. Two more were destroyed by Lt Palliser, while Lts Baker, P.J. Sims, O. Lamplough and H.W. Ross accounted for one each. Unfortunately, Sims failed to return from this fight.

On 30 October, the bomb-carrying SE 5s of No 2 Squadron AFC joined other aircraft in an attack on Rebaix airfield. The bombs were dropped from a very low altitude – sometimes as low as twenty feet – destroying several hangars and buildings as well as three LVG two-seaters parked nearby. The raid was escorted by eleven Snipes of No 4 Squadron, but no enemy aircraft were sighted.

There was no respite for the German Flying Corps now, a fact made clear in an account of the last days of one embattled fighter unit, *Jasta* 356.

> 'The changes of aerodrome grew more frequent. The *Staffel* found nowhere to rest. At the end of October the Flanders autumn sent its fogs. A closed blanket of dirty grey clouds hung at 200 metres, and the wind tore fluttering swathes from its edges . . . visibility was limited to something less than 500 metres.
>
> 'The front line changed every day. Spying eyes saw the flat-brimmed English or American helmets rising out of trenches which had contained the round German ones the day before. Every day there was heavy fighting in the air. The *Jagdstaffel* pushed along the trenches at 20 metres' height – where were the friends and where the foes? The fights were bitter ones, for it seemed as if everyone wanted to put forth his last reserves of energy. English reconnaissance machines harassed the German retreat wherever they could. The numerical superiority of the enemy increased from day to day. Eight to one were the usual odds now. The English and Americans fought ruthlessly, for they had inexhaustible reserves of men and materials.
>
> 'The brown Fokkers fought as they had never fought before. The pilots hardly slept; they hardly ate; they just flew and fought or changed their aerodrome. And with them went their mechanics.
>
> 'The never-ending stream of regiments still flowed on. But no new men came to join them. Likewise it often happened that men who went home on leave did not return to the front.
>
> 'On November 1st and 2nd all available machines were concentrated in the northernmost corner of Flanders. Heavy bombers, scout and reconnaissance machines stood ready to take off. A huge air raid on England had been planned. It was a raid which would destroy everything that could be destroyed. It was to be a work of destruction on such a colossal scale that it would far exceed anything hitherto done in this war. But it remained only a plan . . . '

The battles of late October saw an extraordinary act of valour by a Canadian pilot, Major W.G. Barker. It is, perhaps, best told in the terse language of the official communique.

> 'October 27th. Major Barker, who was on a refresher course from England with 201 Sqn, while on patrol on a Sopwith Snipe, attacked an EA two-seater at 21,000 feet over the Foret de Mormal, and the EA broke up in the air. He was then fired at from below and wounded by a Fokker biplane, and fell into a spin, from which he pulled out in the middle of a formation of fifteen Fokkers, two of which he attacked indecisively. He then got on the tail of a third, which he shot down in flames from a range of ten yards. He was again wounded and fainted; on recovering, he regained control of his machine and was attacked by a large formation of EA, one of

which he shot down in flames from close range. He was then hit in the left elbow, which was shattered, and he again fainted, his machine falling to 12,000 feet before he recovered. Another large formation of EA then attacked him and, noticing heavy smoke coming from his machine, he believed it to be on fire, so tried to ram a Fokker. He opened fire on it from close range, and the EA fell in flames. Major Barker then dived to within a few thousand feet of the ground, but found his retreat cut off by eight EA, at which he fired a few bursts and succeeded in shaking them off, returning to our lines a few feet from the ground, where he finally crashed near our balloons. During the latter part of the combat Major Barker was without the use of both his legs and one arm, and brought his machine back with the thumb switch.'

Bill Barker, who already had forty-six victories to his credit – most of them gained while flying on the Italian Front – was twenty-four years old. His decorations included the DSO and Bar, MC and two Bars, the *Croix de Guerre* and the Italian Cross of Valour. To these, now, was added the Victoria Cross.

Barker survived his serious injuries only to lose his life in 1930, while working as a test pilot.

The spell of poor weather that had shrouded Flanders in low cloud lifted at last on 4 November. On that day, No 2 Squadron AFC formed part of a force that carried out a highly successful attack on Wattines airfield. The raid, which was escorted by No 4 Squadron AFC and the Bristol Fighters of No 88 Squadron RAF, was hotly contested by the enemy, and in the running battle that developed six Fokkers were shot down. But it was a bad day for No 4 Squadron: Lieutenant Goodson was hit by anti-aircraft fire, crashing into the canal at Tournai, and Lt C.W. Rhodes was shot down in combat, both men surviving to become prisoners. They were luckier than Captain T.C.R. Baker and Lts Palliser and P.W. Symons, all of whom were shot down and killed.

It was a hard loss for the Australians to bear, with the end of the war so near. The Germans were now in full retreat through Belgium, and in the days that followed both Australian squadrons were engaged in attacks on enemy forces near Ghislenghien, rolling stock at Enghien and on Croisette airfield. No opposition was encountered in the air, and so the Snipes of No 4 Squadron came down to join the SEs in strafing attacks. The last offensive sortie by the Australian Snipes was carried out on 10 November, when enemy columns were strafed in the Enghien area.

The good order of the German Army was now in a state of collapse, morale being further undermined by revolutionary movements. *Leutnant* Olden, commanding *Jasta* 356, had a nasty experience with one such faction, as the unit's history recounts.

'On November 8th the chief was summoned to HQ . . . he returned on the 9th, with a face as white as a sheet and staring eyes. His sword-knot was missing; his uniform and his right epaulette were torn. He looked to be fifty-six years old instead of twenty-six. He left his horrified comrades standing, walked into the office as if in a trance and wrote out the following statement: "On my way back from HQ I was held up by a sergeant in command of infantrymen wearing red armbands and ordered to remove my sword-knot, brevet and shoulder-straps. When I refused, the men made a physical assault on me. In my own defence I drew my Browning, fired and wounded the sergeant in the arm."'

Olden paraded the *Staffel* – eight pilots and seventy-eight ground personnel – and informed them that the aircraft were to be flown to Germany. The Dutch government had given them permission to fly through Holland to Krefeld, then up the Rhine to Mainz. He then informed the men that a German Republic had been proclaimed in Berlin, and that the Kaiser was seeking refuge in neutral Holland. Before anyone could stop him, Olden drew his pistol and shot himself through the head.

In the last hours of the war, the weather was fair but misty. During the night of 10/11 November, No 214 Squadron's Handley Page O/400s dropped 112 bombs on Louvain railway sidings, the crews reporting many direct hits. Some of the bombs hit an ammunition train, causing explosions and fires all over the sidings.

At eleven o'clock in the morning of 11 November, 1918, the armistice came into effect. Forty-five minutes later, an RE 8 observation aircraft touched down at Auchy. Its crew, Captains H.L. Tracy and S.F. Davison, reported that no enemy aircraft had been seen; British troops were in Mons, where the British Expeditionary Force's long retreat had started more than four years earlier, and enemy AA fire was nil.

On the Western Front, at last, all was quiet.

Different people greeted the news of the armistice in different ways. For the Richthofen *Jagdgeschwader*, the end of the most terrible war in history was recorded by a brief note written by its commander, Hermann Göring.

> 'November 11th. Armistice. *Geschwader* assembled at Darmstadt in bad weather. Fog.'

There was no doubting the jubilation experienced by Captain John Pattern, now instructing with an artillery observation school at Old Sarum in Wiltshire. The three flights entered in his log book for 11 November are followed by the remarks 'Aerobatics – aerobatics – aerobatics – PEACE DAY!'

Captain Cecil Lewis, formerly of the celebrated No 56 Squadron but now with No 152 near Lille, had mixed feelings. He wrote:

> 'I confess to a feeling of anti-climax, even to a momentary sense of regret. We were a new squadron, fresh overseas, we wanted – particularly the new pilots – to justify our existence, to carry out in action the thing we had been training for. Moreover, when you have been living a certain kind of life for four years, living as part of a single-minded and united effort, its sudden cessation leaves your roots in the air, baffled and, for the moment, disgruntled. But the readjustment was rapid and soon we began to explore the possibilities of peace. Where should we go? What should we do?'

The same thoughts undoubtedly passed through the minds of Georges Madon, and Charles Nungesser, and René Fonck on that November day. Madon had gained his forty-first and last victory on 30 October, when he destroyed a Fokker D VII flown by *Feldwebel* Ludwig Pfluger near Dizy-le-Gros. He remained in the *Aviation Militaire* and was posted to Tunisia, where he was killed during an Armistice Day air display at Tunis on 11 November 1924. The cause of the accident was never established. He is buried in the cemetery at Bagneux, on the outskirts of Paris.

Nungesser, still suffering bouts of poor health, formed his own aviation company after the war, as did many other hopefuls whose only trade was flying. On 8 May 1927, together with Francois Coli, his navigator, he took off from Paris in an attempt to cross the Atlantic from east to west. The aircraft was a Levasseur named *L'Oiseau Blanc* (The White Bird) in memory of the *Cigognes*, and on its side it carried a macabre symbol, derived from a degree in Freemasonry, that was Nungesser's personal symbol, one which had been painted on his fighter during the war: a heart bearing a skull and crossbones, a coffin and two funeral candles.

The aircraft took off safely, and as soon as it was airborne Nungesser jettisoned its undercarriage – a measure designed to save weight and cut down drag, for the Levasseur would have to battle against the prevailing westerly wind. A small armada of aircraft accompanied it

Above and Above Right: RAF personnel of No 85 Squadron with captured Fokker D VIIs, November 1918.

as far as the English Channel, then it continued alone until it was lost to sight against the western sky.

It vanished without trace, somewhere over the Atlantic. All that remained of it was its undercarriage, preserved today in France's *Musée de l'Air*.

As for René Fonck: in the forty-eight hours between 30 October and 1 November France's ace of aces destroyed six enemy aircraft, the last a Halberstadt C II which, crewed by *Leutnant* Fischer and *Unteroffizier* Jeromin, was dropping propaganda leaflets on French positions at Vouziers. It was his seventy-fifth victory.

After the war, Fonck took up a career in civil aviation. In the spring of 1920, while attending a banquet in Stockholm to mark the occasion of the founding of a Swedish airline, he had a curious experience. One evening after dinner, he received a telephone call from someone who would only identify himself as a former member of the Richthofen *Geschwader*. The caller turned out to be Hermann Göring, its last commander, who like many others had left the chaos of post-war Germany and for some time had been eking out a living by giving pleasure flights. Now, desperately anxious to find a job in commercial aviation, he asked Fonck to put in a good word for him. The French ace, anxious to help a fellow pilot and former adversary, did not hesitate. He dropped a word in the appropriate quarter, and Göring got a job with the new airline.

Years later, this act of kindness was to have unforeseen repercussions. Following the Franco-German armistice of June 1940, Fonck – who then had the rank of lieutenant-colonel in the *Armée de l'Air* – was summoned to Vichy by Marshal Philippe Pétain, who asked the pilot if he would visit Göring, exploit his old contact, and try to sound out Hitler's intentions with regard to the future of Vichy France.

As Pétain's emissary, Fonck visited Göring several times during the next two years, and the two became friendly. In 1945, however, when the leaders of Vichy France were placed on trial, some of the mud thrown at them inevitably stuck on Fonck. Almost overnight, he fell from his status as a national hero to something approaching that of a criminal. Old friends avoided him, forgetting his former exploits – just as France conveniently forgot that Pétain himself had been the 'Hero of Verdun' in the former war. And so René Fonck died in Paris on 18 June 1953, a broken and embittered man, his star eclipsed by the spite and bitterness of those who knew nothing of the wind in the wires, or the taut drumming of fabric on an aircraft's wing, or the cameraderie that exists between flying men, no matter what their nationality.

He was fifty-nine years old. His remains lie in Saulcy-sur-Meurthe, the village where he was born, surrounded by the wooded slopes of the Vosges mountains.

Select Bibliography

Bruce, J.M. *War Planes of the First World War: Fighters, vols I-III* (Macdonald & Co, London, 1965-69)

Cole, Christopher (Ed) *Royal Air Force 1918* (William Kimber, London 1968)

Cole, Christopher and Cheeseman, E. F. *The Air Defence of Great Britain, 1914-1918* (Putnam, London, 1984)

Cross, Robin *The Bombers* (Bantam Press, London, 1987)

Danel Raymond and Cuny, Jean *l'Aviation Francaise de Bombardement et de Renseignement, 1918-1940* (Editiones Lariviere, Paris 1978)

Franks, Norman *Aircraft versus Aircraft* (Bantam Press, London, 1986)

Gray, Peter and Thetford, Owen *German Aircraft of the First World War* (Putnam, London, 1962)

Hall, N.S. *The Balloon Buster* (Corgi, London, 1967)

Hegener, Henri *Fokker – the Man and His Aircraft* (Harleyford, Letchworth, 1961)

Jackson, Robert *Fighter Pilots of World War 1* (Arthur Barker, London, 1977)

Jullian, Marcel *la Grande Bataille dans les Airs* (Presses de la Cite, Paris, 1967)

Kahnert, M.E. *Jagdstaffel 356* (John Hamilton, London, 1936)

Lewis, Cecil *Sagittarius Rising* (Peter Davies, London, 1936)

Lewis, Peter *The British Bomber Since 1914* (Putnam, London, 1980)

Neumann, G.P. *Die Deutschen Luftstreitkräfte im Weltkriege* (Berlin, 1922)

Nowarra, H.J. and Brown, K.S.: *Von Richthofen and the Flying Circus* (Harleyford, Letchworth, 1958)

Raleigh, Sir Walter and Jones, H.A. *The War in the Air* (6 vols, OUP, 1922-37)

Rickenbacker, E.V. *Fighting the Flying Circus* (Doubleday, New York, 1965)

Saunders, Hilary St G: *Per Ardua* (Oxford University Press, London, 1944)

Index

GENERAL